D0366939

BUILDING TOGETHER

▶**Developing
Your Blueprint
for Congregational
Youth Ministry**

▶**Carol Duerksen**

**Foreword by Roland D. Martinson
Preface by Abe Bergen**

"It is simply written so that any youth sponsor from any congregation in North America can read it and get a handle on what congregational youth ministry is all about."
—*Gareth Brandt, instructor at Columbia Bible College, Abbotsford, B.C.*

Building Together is designed for real congregations in a great many real places. Readers are helped to better understand what it is like to be a teenager growing up in post-modern society. They will learn ways to join youth in working out their life and faith, strengthened by the power of God as it is mediated by the community of faith.
—*from the Foreword by Roland D. Martinson*

Faith & Life
Resources

A Division of Mennonite Publishing House

*Scottdale, Pennsylvania
Newton, Kansas
Waterloo, Ontario
Winnipeg, Manitoba*

*Building Together: Developing Your Blueprint
for Congregational Youth Ministry*

Copyright © 2001 by Faith & Life Resources, Newton, KS 67114, Scottdale, PA 15683.

All rights reserved. No part of this publication may be reproduced, stored in a retrieval system, or transmitted, in any form or by any means, electronic, mechanical, photocopying, recording, or otherwise, without the written permission of the publishers.

Library of Congress Control Number: 2001126248

International Standard Book Number 0-8361-9189-7

This book is based on *Blueprint for Congregational Youth Ministry* by Lavon J. Welty (Newton: Faith & Life Press, 1988).

Cover and interior design by Gwen M. Stamm
Photo credit Merrill R. Miller and Marilyn Nolt

Printed in the United States of America

1   2   3   4   5   6   06   05   04   03   02   01

Blueprint of Contents

Foreword

THESE CHANGING times remind Christians today of the difficult task the Israelites faced as they were about to enter the "promised land"—a land filled with "milk and honey" and people serving other gods. God's words to them are right on the mark for the task of passing on the faith today:

> Hear O Israel: The Lord is our God, the Lord alone. You shall love the Lord your God with all your heart, and with all your soul, and with all your might. Keep these words that I am commanding you today in your heart. Recite them to your children and talk about them when you are at home and when you are away, when you lie down and when you rise (Deut. 6:4-7 NRSV).

How does one pass on the faith in difficult times? The Bible asserts: focus on the living, present, and active God; nurture in each other a strong faith at the very center of personal and communal living; and forever keep this God and this dynamic faith in the forefront of your minds and practices, so that all of life becomes the laboratory where faith is taught, explored, and claimed among all generations.

Building Together develops these biblical commitments and practices into an effective model of youth ministry that boldly faces the challenges of the 21st century. It is Christ-centered, steadily focused on the gracious, transforming power of God. It engages the whole congregation in shared ministry not only with youth but with children and adults as well. Families are called to be primary nurturers of faith. Community and congregational life are arenas in which faith is presented and worked out.

This book sees youth ministry first and foremost as concern and care for persons. Even as relationships are at the heart of vital faith, so relationships are the fiber of this model. The best elements of both peer and intergenerational relationships are called forth. Youth and adults stand shoulder to shoulder in compassion and service as they care for the world in the name of Jesus Christ. The gifts of teenagers are recognized and called into leadership within the congregation and into God's mission in the community.

Building Together is designed for real congregations in a great many real places. Readers are helped to better understand what it is like to be a teenager growing up in post-modern society. They will learn ways to join youth in working out their life and faith, strengthened by the power of God as it is mediated by the community of faith. One finds here the tools through which a congregation can custom design ministry for a particular community, with its own unique young people.

Building Together envisions an intergenerational team of leaders guiding their congregation and its families into an honest engagement with their youth. With God in the lead and this wise book as their guide, congregational youth ministry teams will have an interesting adventure passing on the faith, shaping the values, and making disciples of a new generation!

Roland D. Martinson
Professor of Pastoral Care, Luther Seminary
St. Paul, Minnesota

Preface

AN INVITATION to a diverse group of 12 Mennonite youth leaders from across Canada and the USA might have read: "Your mission, should you choose to accept it, is to discern the kind of printed youth ministry resource needed to equip adults to minister effectively to youth in Anabaptist congregations in the new millennium." Instead, the purpose of the consultation was stated with less drama and intrigue: "To update/revise *Blueprint for Congregational Youth Ministry.*" Participants were given articles and books to read and invited to Tall Oaks Conference Center in Linwood, Kansas, December 3-4, 1999.

Blueprint had served Mennonite and Church of the Brethren congregations for more than a decade as a guide for those working with youth. The group at the consultation was divided—some wanted a completely new resource while others felt minor changes were needed. Though excellent discussions prevailed, it took a further meeting in May 2000 to finalize the plan.

The May meeting in Hampton, Virginia, consisted of 30 members of the Youth Ministry Council, a network of Mennonite conference youth ministers. A few members of the council had been part of an exciting 1987 book-length writing project that would articulate youth ministry from an Anabaptist perspective. *Blueprint for Congregational Youth Ministry* was released in 1988, replacing the articles and pamphlets that had previously guided youth leaders in Mennonite and Church of the Brethren congregations.

Author Lavon Welty brought a decade of experience and learning to the project. His insights were enriched by the wisdom and experiences of youth ministry practitioners from across Canada and the USA. It became the foundation of youth ministry for Anabaptist churches. *Blueprint*, as it was affectionately known, was tagged as a textbook for college and seminary courses, and read as a reference book by pastors and youth leaders.

Blueprint was more of a "why" book than a "how to" book. The "how to" part was fleshed out when *41 Ways to a Better Youth Group* by Mike Bogard (Faith & Life Press, 1996) was published. This book, addressing "Leadership, Worship, Community and Mission," provides practical ideas for improving congregational youth ministry. It continues to be an accessible resource for volunteers and professionals alike. Add to that Steve Ropp's mentoring manual, *One on One* (1993), and you have the makings of a youth ministry library.

Is *Blueprint* relevant enough to reprint? Many excellent youth ministry resources have been published since 1988. One I found provocative and challenging was *The Coming Revolution in Youth Ministry* by Mark Senter III (SP Publication, 1992). In this significant book, Senter sketched a history of youth ministry in the USA and challenged readers to search for the paradigm (model of ministry) that would best serve youth and congregations in the future.

His thesis is that youth ministry, as we know it, is rapidly running out of steam. He identified three fifty-year "revolutions" (cycles) that had taken place in youth ministry. Each cycle brought a new approach. As societal conditions changed, one cycle ended and new initiatives were required to reach youth for Christ.

The Sunday school and the YMCA dominated the first 50-year cycle, "youth ministry as education" (1824-1875). Both movements originated in England, came to the eastern USA, spread westward, and later northward to Canada. Public funding for schools brought this cycle to an end. Education became accessible to all, not limited to what was available through churches.

The second cycle, "youth ministry as socialization" (1881-1925), was a by-product of urbanization, when many young adults flocked to the cities to grab the new jobs that sprouted during this period of industrialization. Christian Endeavor became one of the main ways to "protect young people from the evil influences of the city" and keep them accountable and growing in their walk with God.

In the third cycle, "youth ministry as professionalization" (1935-1987), we saw the proliferation of parachurch ministries, such as Young Life and Youth for Christ, and the emergence of youth ministry staff positions in denominational offices and congregations. For example, in 1935 H. A. Fast became the first part-time youth secretary for the General Conference Mennonite Church. There has been a youth ministry staff person at the denominational office ever since.

It is coincidental that Senter saw the third cycle of youth ministry coming to an end in 1987, the same year the Youth Ministry Council was discussing the draft manuscript for *Blueprint*. Was *Blueprint* the last gasp of the current cycle or would it be the cutting edge of the future? I am convinced the latter is the case. Welty's *Blueprint*, and now this update of it by Carol Duerksen, reflect a future paradigm that will characterize youth ministry during the fourth cycle.

Since first reading Senter's book in 1992, I have been on a quest for the new paradigm. I speculated and promoted some of my "theories."

Mentoring—For a time I felt "mentoring" was the key to the future. Mentoring, the pairing of an adult and a teen, is a simple ministry approach that can be as successful in a congregation of one or two youth as in a congregation of 100+ youth. The fact that the Mennonite church developed mentoring into a congregational program (*Side by Side: A Mentoring Guide for Congregational Youth Ministry* by Lavon Welty, Faith & Life Press, 1989) was an exciting prospect. Yet it never took off in a definitive way, even when Youth Specialties and David C. Cook adapted it in their *One Kid at a Time* resource kit.

Family-Based Youth Ministry—When *Family-Based Youth Ministry* (Mark DeVries, InterVarsity Press, 1994) was published, I was temporarily convinced that *it* would become the new paradigm. If we better equipped parents to pass on the faith to their children, if we fostered a stronger partnership between home and congregation, we'd enhance youth ministry.

Praise and worship services—Praise and worship services can engage youth—heart, mind, soul, and strength—in worshiping God. In some communities, such services are drawing hundreds and even thousands of youth for weekly worship celebrations.

Spirituality Project—Another recent emphasis is the Spirituality Project that began at San Francisco Theological Seminary with codirectors Mark Yaconelli and Andy Dreitcer. In this approach, ancient spiritual practices such as *Awareness Examen* and *Lectio Divina* tapped into a resurgence of spirituality in North America.

Multiple strategies—When no single strategy seemed to emerge as the best way, I considered the possibility that several paradigms might be the future. Rapid societal changes could result in a different paradigm dominating for 10-year intervals, rather than one paradigm for 50 years. This did not materialize.

Then I noticed a common thread in the new approaches: the isolation of youth from the adult world. Writers and speakers lamented the segregation, concerned that more time was being spent with peers than in intergenerational contexts. "Children are raising children" headlines screamed. The isolation of children and youth was becoming a major problem in contemporary society. Twenty or thirty years ago youth had intergenerational contacts. Now with both parents working outside the home youth were left to themselves, even to the point of being abandoned. Societal institutions, including the church, were becoming more age segregated.

It appeared that the greatest need in youth ministry was the integration of youth and adults. Efforts in youth ministry that were effective were those striving to be wholistic. Intergenerational connections bringing youth and adults together in a mentoring program fit this bill. A stronger partnership between home and congregation hit the nail on the head, as did faith-shaping worship for adults and youth alike.

Welty (*Blueprint,* 1988) made two main points in his book. First, youth ministry must be integrated into the entire life of the congregation. Along with others, he noticed responsibility for youth was often relegated to a few volunteers known as sponsors or leaders, or in the case of larger congregations, the youth pastor. He contended the youth group had become a parallel congregation, with adult sponsors serving as a precarious bridge between congregation and youth group.

Others share his analysis and identify the problem as the one-eared Mickey Mouse phenomena (*The Godbearing Life* by Kenda Creasy Dean and Ron Foster, p. 31; *Family-Based Youth Ministry* by Mark DeVries, p. 42). The danger in separating youth from the rest of the congregation is that youth graduate out of the church when they graduate out of the youth group.

Welty's second point was that youth ministry efforts within the congregation needed to be coordinated, not fragmented—for example there was little communication between the Sunday school and the youth group. Thus he proposed rebuilding congregational youth ministry to integrate youth into the entire life of the congregation, coordinating all ministry efforts through a planning team.

Wholistic ministry is the vision of *Blueprint* (1988). Welty's two main emphases are as relevant today as they were in 1988. The commitment to wholistic ministry will characterize the next "revolution" (or cycle) of youth ministry. Youth must be restored to their rightful place in the church community rather than relegated to a peer group that runs parallel with their congregation.

In *Building Together: Developing Your Blueprint for Congregational Youth Ministry*, Duerksen has retained the essential components of the *Blueprint* model while making the application of the theory more accessible to the reader. We need to recover a wholistic approach to youth ministry, which counters our fragmented, age-segregated society. *Building Together* continues that counter-cultural direction, a journey *Blueprint* began in 1988.

Abe Bergen
Director of Youth Ministry
General Conference Mennonite Church
December 7, 2000

Introduction

THE BIG WHITE three-story barn nestled comfortably into the Kansas hillside, as if it had been there long enough to relax, rest, and just let life come along as it may.

"It's a wonderful barn," I told my husband, Maynard, as we contemplated buying the farm.

"I bet it could tell wonderful stories," he agreed. "We'll have to ask the former owners about it if we buy this place."

We bought the farm. We asked the people who grew up on this farm to tell us about the barn. We heard about the dairy stanchions in the lower level north side, the big fork and rope that brought hay up to the hay loft, the specially constructed elevator that allowed the farmer to dump grain into a pit and then bring it up to the bins high above on the third floor.

The stories were nice—even interesting. But we didn't have dairy cows. We didn't have grain to dump. And we didn't have loose hay to move into a hayloft.

Sure, we liked the character the barn brought to the yard, its sense of history. But practically speaking, it didn't serve our needs. We are "postmodern farmers"—people who live on a farmyard because we like the feel of being in the country. We enjoy having a few animals around for fun, not for a livelihood. Maybe we need a new barn, we thought. One of those beautiful shiny metal structures like the other postmodern farmers have on their farmyards.

One day, something happened as we were standing inside the old barn.

"You know, if we'd clean up the hayloft, it would make a great place for the youth group to have parties," I said.

"Yeah, and if I'd build some stalls downstairs we could put the horses in there when it's cold," Maynard agreed.

One thing led to another, and another, and another. Years after we first saw that old barn, it still rests against its Kansas hillside. The structure has been reinforced and spruced up. The barn's the same barn, but if you were to open the door, what a difference you'd see. The difference is what's happening *inside* that old barn.

The Old Youth Ministry Cow

For many of us growing up in the church, youth ministry has been nearly synonymous with "youth group." And for a good number of us, the youth group did a satisfactory job of holding us "within the fold" of our congregation. We found the peer relationships fulfilling, the service trips meaningful, and the sessions worth attending. Our identity with our congregation was tied to our involvement with the youth group.

Congregational members also viewed youth group as the place where youth received most of their experience with the church body. Sunday school was another setting, and at some point catechetical instruction or membership class. The adults that youth came into the most significant contact with were their youth group sponsors and Sunday school teachers. Beyond that, their connection with the church family, worship, committees, and activities was somewhat limited. They would "grow up" into those roles. For the time being, the youth group was their focal point.

Today, that model for youth ministry is a dying cow.

New Life Inside the Barn

Our church congregations are still made up of people who come together to worship God. The outside structure has remained the same for many years. But the lives of the people on the inside have been changing. The difference between what it was like for us as teenagers, and what teens are experiencing today is perhaps the most dramatic. The exploding world of the Internet, year-round sports op-portunities, summer camps, increased pressure to make good grades to get into college, the importance of having a job, the media, and the outside influences on how youth develop their values—these are some of the biggest differences between "then" and "now."

In some cases, the traditional approach to youth group is still working in this changing environment. But in most congregations, it is no longer enough to keep youth interested and involved. There are too many other things clamoring for their attention.

Does our ministry to youth need a new barn? Or is it possible that it isn't a new structure that we need, but a new way of looking at what happens inside the existing structure?

This book is a blueprint for the remodeling, if you will, of traditional youth ministry. But before we get out the floor plans, let's catalog what else we visualized for the barn's future.

Who Will Live Here?

When I said I'd love to see the hayloft cleaned up, and Maynard said he could build stalls in the lower floor, the ideas began to fly.

"I'd like a place for the llamas to come in out of the weather," I said.

"I want some nests for chickens and ducks to set on their eggs," Maynard added.

"We need a dry place to store a few square bales of alfalfa for the goats," I noted.

"It'd be good to have a pen to bring a cow and calf in during the winter," Maynard mused.

"We don't need the big grain bins, but we need a place to store a few sacks of feed," I realized. "We could put a door on one of the bins and maybe a ceiling."

"And use it for a tack room too," Maynard added, catching the idea. "A place to keep the saddle and halters."

Over the next months, our words rang with the smack of hammer against nails. Our ideas positioned two-by-fours and planks of wood. The old barn felt new life moving inside, and it smiled.

People Before Program

Before the barn could be rebuilt, Maynard and I looked at who would be using it. Before those of us involved in youth ministry can look at a blueprint on "how to do it," we need to look at the lives we hope to shape. Our fundamental concern is building the life of each youth. And while it may be easy to focus on how WE want to shape THEM, it is equally important for the church to think about what it wants to be TO and WITH youth.

Elizabeth O'Conner puts it this way in her book *Eighth Day of Creation* (Word Publishers, 1974).

> The primary purpose of the church is to help us discover our gifts and, in the face of our fears, to hold us accountable for them so that we can enter into the joy of creating. The major obligation of the church to [young people] is to enjoy them and listen to them so that each can grow according to the design which is written into his (or her) being and emerges only under the care and warmth of another life. One of the reasons we experience so much difficulty with our gifts is that parents have thought their chief function in life to be feeding, clothing, and educating the young. However, their really important ministry is to listen to their children and enable them to uncover the special blueprint that is theirs.

What should the church endeavor to be and do with youth? Help them discover their gifts. Enjoy, listen, and learn from them. Help them know that God is reaching out to them. Provide an environment where commitment to Christ is modeled and encouraged. Inspire them to let God's love shine through them and to minister to others. What do we want our youth to be and become? It is our prayer that they will be

- Followers of Jesus
- Integral parts of congregational life
- Ambassadors of healing and hope

Section I of this book will explore the milieu of our youth—their concerns and pressure points, issues and decisions. We will begin to look at the interactions between adults and youth. As we do, we are assessing the "lay of the land"—the building site that will inform our youth ministry blueprint. This section suggests ways to view youth and relate to them, so that what we develop will be a blueprint specific to youth ministry.

Section II will discuss what we as a church have to offer youth. Our interaction with youth has as its foundation our faith, and occurs in the context of the congregation. Our mission in relating with young people is to invite them into a personal relationship with

It is just as important for a church to think about what it
wants to be **to** and **with** youth as what it wants youth
to **be** and **become**.

Christ, encourage them to be active participants in a church community, and empower them to bring healing and hope to the world.
The blueprint is now not only of a barn, if you will, but a certain
kind of barn.

Section III of this book explores eleven settings where youth can
learn how to build the framework of their lives. This is where we put
the blueprint into action. This is where we build together.

SECTION 1

Where They Are and Where You Fit In

CHAPTER 1

Decisions, Decisions

ANDREA VOTH knew she was going to college. No question about that. But *which* college? She visited her "short list" and tried to decide. Her parents drove hundreds of miles with her as they visited six different colleges—Goshen and Earlham in Indiana. Lake Forest in Illinois. Grinnell in Iowa. McAllister and Carlton in Minnesota.

They listened to her. Made suggestions. Prayed. Hoped. They knew that only one person could make the decision, and no matter how strongly they felt about one choice over the other, it wouldn't be their choice. It would be Andrea's.

Andrea wanted and listened to her parents' input. She weighed what each college had to offer. She weighed its distance from home. She weighed how she felt when she walked on the campus and met the staff. She considered all the factors, and she made her choice.

Even as we in the church decide how we want to help shape the lives of our youth, we must acknowledge that they are decision-makers in their own right. Their decisions—not ours—are the structural elements, the wood and brick, of their identity and life-building project. Like Andrea's parents, we can guide, suggest, hope, and pray them through this crucial time in their lives. But we can't do it for them. If we do, chances are they will find other opportunities to exert their choice-making, and those may have very negative outcomes.

The college decision—if and which—is just one of many that teenagers face. Others include:

• *Family life.* How will she relate to her parents and siblings? Will she cooperate willingly in household and family chores? How will she respond to parental authority and her own need for independence? Will she share the same values and attitudes that are important to her parents? How will she feel about her family's traditions and history?

• *Peer relationships.* What will he look for in friends? Will his values and beliefs be shaped by his friends, and is he choosing friends that will be positive influences in his life? How will he relate to peers who are different—those from families with significantly more or less income, from another culture or ethnic group, or those with physical, emotional, or mental challenges?

• *Moral issues.* Will she cheat? Will honesty be a high value for her? What values will guide her attitudes and behaviors toward the natural environment and material possessions?

• *The church and faith.* Will he choose to commit himself to Christ? Will he be active in a church congregation? Will he own for himself and base his lifestyle on his denomination's beliefs on issues such as peace and nonresistance? Will he apply the teachings of the church in his daily life? How will he respond when he sees that not all members of the church live out what the church teaches?

• *Sexuality.* How will he deal with the physical urges that cry out for expression, and which are often stimulated by the blatant sexual themes in movies, music, and magazines? How will he relate to members of the opposite sex, both in casual and in dating relationships? How will he handle the possible discovery that he or friends of his are gay or lesbian? How will he feel about his body image? How will he respond to the stereotypes society wraps around males and females?

• *Use of time.* What will her priorities be for her time? Sports? The computer and the Internet? Schoolwork? Dating and friendships? A job? Church involvement? Family? Personal and spiritual growth? When push comes to shove in her busy life, what will be shoved aside?

• *Use of money.* Will he work in order to have money for college, a car, CDs? Will he give to the church? Will money be important in order to have the clothes with the right name? How will he respond to youth who don't have money? How will he differentiate between needs and wants?

• *The future.* Will he go to college? If so, will it be a church or secular school? Or will he go to a trade school? Get a job after high school? Go into a service assignment? Do nothing? How will he support himself? Will he live at home or establish his own household? Will he marry? How will he choose a life partner? How would he respond if his country called him to war?

• *Worldview.* How does she respond to the needs of people around the world? Does she feel responsible for caring for the natural world? Is she concerned about the well-being of all people of the earth regardless of nationality, race, or culture? Is her approach to life essentially competitive or cooperative? What will be her attitude toward the violence that exists in society?

• *Support system.* Where will he receive the support to make these decisions? Parents, siblings, grandparents, extended family members? Will his support group be peers or a mix of people from different generations? What role will the church family play?

This list of questions, though not exhaustive, feels exhausting when we realize how many issues youth face during their teen years and early 20s. Certainly some of the decisions are carried into adulthood, and some may never be fully resolved, but is it any wonder that the lives of youth are fraught with emotional ups and downs? Anyone who has ever built or remodeled a house knows the stress factors (both emotional and architectural) involved. Our youth are building the house of their lives.

Shaping Identity

I'll never forget "the rope incident" of my teenage years. I'd had a fight with my parents about something that was hugely important to me at the time—so important that when I didn't get my way, I stormed upstairs to my bedroom and let them know I would not be coming down to see them again, ever.

While contemplating life in my bedroom, I realized I didn't really want to stay up there forever, but neither did I want to go down the stairs and have to walk past the objects of my frustration. The solution? Escape down the "fire rope" tied to my bedroom closet.

I'd never shimmied down a rope before, and the thought of escaping from my upstairs room via a rope meant to be used only in emergencies intrigued me. I found a pair of red woolen winter gloves to prevent rope burn, threw the rope out the window, and eased myself out. This wasn't going to be easy, but I was going to do it, yes sirree.

I hit the ground with jubilation. I'd shown them, yes I did!

And then, pleased and proud of my feat, I strutted into the house, grinning from ear to ear, to tell my parents about my accomplishment.

Teens experience a huge need for independence, matched only by their equally large desire for approval and affirmation. I hated the authority my parents were exerting over me, I "escaped" to prove my independence, and then I couldn't wait to hear their approval of my brave feat.

Teens are experimenting. Shaping their identity. Deciding "Who am I?" "Who will I be?" Youth who don't carry out this task successfully as adolescents can develop a confused sense of role that permeates the rest of their lives.

I have often wondered why wonderful families who adopt babies often go through really tough times with them as teenagers and into their adult years. A friend of mine shared with me that she scheduled appointments with her adopted son and his school counselor when he was just seven years old to process his adoption and his feelings about being given up by his birth parents. The idea is that if he can process those feelings early, the chances are better that when he goes through puberty and takes a long look at who he is and is becoming, the "homework" he's done in that part of his life will keep him from the trauma many adopted teens go through.

In the process of deciding who they are and who they are becoming, youth often experiment with a variety of ideals, behaviors, and involvements. Their sense of risk is underdeveloped and decision-making is often trial and error. Sometimes the outcome is successful and they receive praise and high-fives for what they've done. Other times the consequences of bad choices are criticism, reprimands, punishment, or even injury and death.

Adults relating to youth find these years both exhilarating and exhausting. One moment you're having a conversation with what seems to be a mature young adult, and the next moment you're wondering what he was thinking when he had sex with his girlfriend. During the day you're so proud of your youth on their service trip, and at night you're gonna kill them if they don't stop talking and making loud body noises when they are supposed to be going to sleep.

Youth are "in process." My husband and I remark on this every year as we watch the freshmen come into our youth group. The contrast in maturity level (generally speaking) between the freshmen and seniors is the best proof we have that this identity-shaping is happening, and it's happening because of and in spite of our involvement with them. It will happen whether or not we or anyone else at our church intersects with their lives during this crucial time, but our congregation wants to be a part of the youth-in-process as much as we can while giving them the space they need to become the people God intends them to be.

Hand-holding and Finger-pointing

Kenda Creasy Dean and Ron Foster, in their book *The Godbearing Life*, highlight their observation of a mother and her toddler daughter in a park. As the two-year-old navigated her way over the grassy terrain, the mother gently held her fingers, allowing the youngster a "controlled wandering." From time to time, the mother would point to a tree, bird, or flower. The little girl would stop, giggle, point, sound the word her mother said to her, and then move on her self-made path.

Our role with youth is similar—while youth meander through their identity-shaping years, we hold hands and point fingers. Dean and Foster describe several scenarios of interaction between youth and adults—sitting up late with a girl as she pours out her sadness over a broken relationship, hanging out at Pizza Hut and "just talking," listening to a boy as he begins to tell about his parents' divorce, praying with a sobbing girl who thinks no one likes her, playing video games and hearing snatches of a junior high boy's struggle to be accepted, listening as a young man describes his uncertainty about his future.

> What these scenarios have in common is hand-holding, or the ministry of presence. Spiritual hand-holding . . . means listening attentively to the lives and the stories of youth with a particular ear for the God-strand woven into the narrative. . . . Godbearers with youth are called to listen for the whispers of grace in the gaps and in the cracks, to filter out the background noise as much as possible, and to help youth tune into God's voice. Hand-holding means offering a supportive, caring presence that draws youth into the presence of God. In many instances hand-holding is the best gift (and sometimes the only gift) that we have to offer in the name of Christ to the youth with whom we are in ministry. Hand-holding reflects being rather than doing, presence rather than activity.

Look At It This Way

Sometimes it feels like you can read a book on youth ministry and it all sounds so good and "do-able." Then you get involved with kids and the reality bites. What a pain!

Like the time when you spent several sessions talking to your youth class about sex, and the importance of making right choices. Late one night several months later you get a phone call from a sobbing youth group member who thinks she's pregnant.

Or this scenario: The boy you're mentoring has bent your ear about needing money for a car. You help him land a good job. After a month on the job, he gets fired for being late to work too many times.

Or maybe it's your daughter, who insists on buying expensive name-brand clothes, despite your feelings that it is a big waste of money. Now she's taken a job that keeps her away from youth group—just so she can afford the clothes she wants.

Yes, teenagers can be such a pain. You put all of that time and energy into them, and then they make decisions that contradict everything you believe and have tried to teach.

Consider yourself privileged. I do. When a young cool teenage person talks to me—little 47-year-old me—I want to pinch myself. This teen has chosen me to relate to? Me? The woman who doesn't know how to choose the right shoes to wear with a skirt? Me, who's getting wrinkles under her eyes and varicose veins on her legs? Me?

And you know what else? Not only am I privileged to be a teen's friend, I am privileged to be a part of her identity-shaping time of life. Even when I am frustrated with her decisions, I'm there. Bottom line is that I will be there. Holding her hand and pointing my finger.

I don't always do it so well. I can be such a pain to myself when my actions contradict everything I believe and teach. Thank God for grace for us all.

Dean and Foster consider finger-pointing a positive behavior, not pointing at people to pick out flaws. Instead, Godbearing Christians can point youth toward Jesus, toward the Scriptures. They open up the word of God so that it speaks to youth in compelling and accessible ways. Godbearers point to the tradition of the church and toward models and heroes of the faithful. Finger-pointers help youthful travelers know that those who step out on the journey for the long haul fill their backpack with prayer and meditation, worship and service, study and compassion, solitude and community; in short, the spiritual disciplines of the church.

The "New" Teen Years

Some people don't get too worked up about the decisions their youth are facing. "I made it through the teen years, and they will too," is their general approach. "Just let the kids work it out for themselves. I turned out okay and so will they."

The biggest problem with this approach is the difference between their teen years and today. When they were growing up, families (in general) exerted more influence on the youth. Extended families were a part of their support group. The church presented some significant "right and wrong" statements.

The media was an influence, but not what it is today. The Internet didn't exist. Teens weren't as busy as many of them are today.

The other extreme approach to working with youth is to "lay down the law." Try to protect them from the nastiness of society. Shelter them, make sure they are "on the straight and narrow," and make most decisions for them.

Neither approach is adequate. The most important goal is to provide a support system—people, places, and settings where youth come in contact with finger-pointers toward God. These people should be peers as well as elders and children; the places and settings should be inside and outside the church family where they can explore and grow in their faith.

Here's a real-life case of finger-pointing:

Marcus (not his real name) grew up in a committed Christian family. His grandparents were "pillars of the church." His father taught Sunday school occasionally; his mother belonged to an interdenominational Bible study. Marcus wasn't the most dedicated youth group

Lost and Found

[Jesus] said to them, "Why were you searching for me? Did you not know that I must be in my Father's house?" (Luke 2:49)

Jesus is twelve years old. He's just spent three days in the temple with the teachers, asking and answering questions. He is a young man with knowledge and understanding between his ears far beyond his years. When Jesus talks, people listen.

His parents don't know that yet. To them, he's a boy who got himself lost and now they're frantic with worry. They don't know his godly parentage is starting to pull stronger than his earthly mom and dad. They don't know what's going on inside the head of this boy-becoming-a-man, this son of theirs that doesn't belong to them. They don't know, and they aren't ready.

Teens are going to be that way. People who relate to youth are going to struggle with how much to let go and how much to control. Our role is to hold hands, to let go of hands, to point fingers, and to pray them home.

---

member, he wasn't baptized as a teenager, and rumor had it that some of his lifestyle choices weren't what he would have heard taught in Sunday school. Marcus liked to live on the edge.

One Christmas vacation when Marcus was home from the secular university, he struck up a friendship with a schoolmate, Julia. Julia was, in many ways, the opposite of Marcus. She was the "perfect Mennonite daughter." That night Marcus and Julia talked into the wee hours of the morning. She discovered a young man full of enthusiasm for life and a serious side she'd never known existed. He discovered a young woman with a solid faith, a beautiful smile, and an open heart.

Six months later they were engaged.

What happened? Finger-pointing and hand-holding. His parents, grandparents, and mentor prayed for him. His youth group leader made a point of spending time with him at the ski slope. His pastor connected with him when he came home from college. He struck up a deep friendship with a young woman committed to Christ. His life had intertwined with people who, each in his or her own way, shared the love of God. When the timing was right, he responded. No one else could make the decision for him, but they certainly could point the way for when he chose to take the step. Without a doubt, Marcus was blessed with life-changing hand-holding, and it wasn't just between him and Julia.

CHAPTER 2

The Search for Significance

TOM was 15 when he raised his hand in youth group one evening and volunteered to be on the committee to draft the church's new mission statement. Tom was the only one interested in being the youth representative on the committee.

At first, being on the committee felt good. Adults made a point of saying how glad they were to have him on the team. The chairperson of the committee gave him a special welcome at the first meeting and invited him to provide his input from a youth perspective.

But as the weeks and months passed, Tom began complaining about how boring the meetings were. "All I do is sit there for two hours and don't say anything. It wouldn't make any difference if I wasn't there." He didn't feel that he was significant to the committee, and none of the youth he was representing ever talked to him about it. Despite encouragement from committee members who tried to help him get involved in the discussions, Tom participated very little.

Then why did he volunteer? Tom would say he wasn't sure. Subconsciously, his reason for volunteering probably grew out of his search for something that would make him feel significant to the youth in the group. Maybe this would make them notice him.

It didn't, and after the initial affirmation from a few adults wore off, Tom was disillusioned.

Rhonda was frustrated with her lack of a dating life. When she looked at her sister, she saw a slim attractive girl who had lots of dates. When she looked at herself she thought she saw someone fat and ugly. No one else thought that of Rhonda, but she did. So she went on a diet. And when she'd lost ten pounds, and the guys still didn't call, she decided she needed to lose more weight. Before long, she was vomiting after eating in order to lose weight.

Her feelings of being insignificant only increased, and she began exercising to burn calories and lose weight faster. The thinner she got, the more obsessed she was with the idea that she was fat. Her parents and others became deeply alarmed at what was happening to Rhonda. She was diagnosed as being bulimic and anorexic, diseases that could kill her if there wasn't some intervention. The search for significance nearly cost Rhonda her life.

Rob did it all. Football in the fall, basketball in the winter, track in spring, church softball in the summer. He took private trumpet lessons and played in the school symphonic and jazz bands. He volunteered to be the youth group president and was president of the school's honor society. He wasn't satisfied unless his grades got him on the honor roll.

For a while, Rob's parents and friends told him how amazed they were that he could do so much so well. But when their affirmation seemed to lead him to increase his commitments, they began to question his busy schedule and expressed concern over his lack of sleep. Rob got irritated and impatient.

One day a close friend complained that Rob never had time to hang out with him like they used to. His girlfriend said he didn't have time for her anymore. Rob also heard that some were complaining about details falling through the cracks in youth group.

A long talk with his mentor helped Rob see that he didn't have to be superhuman and do everything in order to confirm his value and worth as a person. Rob believed his mentor's words in his head, but deep inside he continued to struggle with questions of whether he was really important to anyone.

Tom, Rhonda, and Rob all had one thing in common that drove them to different responses—the search for significance. "Significance," in this context, is a basic attitude or orientation toward oneself. It is not a fact that can be shown to be true or untrue, nor is it a feeling that can be identified. Significance is confirmed when others affirm the capabilities and accomplishments of a person, and it is damaged by lack of affirmation or communication or an openly critical comment.

Stephen Glenn, a family life education expert, noted in an interview with *Youthworker* magazine that in Western culture the need for significance is "more important than the need to survive. . . . We're the only creatures that we know of that will voluntarily take our own life if we doubt its significance."

Doubting his or her significance is a natural aspect of a young person's passage through the teen years. Unfortunately, at the same time that their bodies are changing, the media is bombarding teens with images of perfect bodies, smooth acne-free faces, and gorgeous hair. As a result, teens like Rhonda go to drastic measures to try to measure up to such images, while others like Rob try to make up for feelings of inadequacy by doing everything. It doesn't help matters when adults get hostile toward teens for some of their actions and attitudes.

How Do You Get "Significance"?

Some teens carry a sense of confidence and contentment with them. It seems they never had to search for their significance—they brought it with them into their teen years. Where did they get it? Why is it easier for some than for others?

One obvious contributing factor is family. A warm, caring, affirming family experience can be the beginning of a solid foundation for a good self-concept. When that foundation is reinforced with words of praise and affirmation from other adults, teachers, and peers, youth have a head start on feeling good about themselves. There are no guarantees, of course, and negative signals from peers can eat away at a seemingly solid foundation very quickly.

Take Kathy, for example. She refuses to go to her high school class reunions. Despite a loving home that laid her the foundation for a good self-concept, she felt that people didn't like her in high school. Despite several close friendships with girls, it is what she remembers of how the guys treated her that keeps her from ever wanting to see them at a reunion. Interestingly enough, her girl friends didn't perceive her treatment by the guys the way she did.

While many factors contribute to a teen's sense of significance, a good self-concept is not something that can be handed to a person. Significance is an inner conviction that is based on what the person believes about him or herself, as well as about the world in which a person lives. If one's inner conviction tends to deny significance, then

"Are These All the Sons You Have?"

In the same way all seven of Jesse's sons were presented to Samuel. But Samuel said to Jesse, "The Lord has not chosen any of these." Then Samuel asked, "Are these all the sons you have?"

"There is still the youngest," Jesse replied. "But he's out in the fields watching the sheep."

"Send for him at once," Samuel said.
(1 Samuel 16:10-11)

It's a wonderful, refreshing story. God's man Samuel is on a mission to the village of Bethlehem—he's supposed to find the next king of Israel. A holy headhunter, if you will. He's been told by God to check out Jesse's sons, and Jesse is more than pleased to cooperate. He presents his eldest, Eliab. Samuel can believe his eyes, but his God-sense has him wondering. His eyes tell him, "It must be this first one—he's tall and handsome, confident, the firstborn son." But God's whispering in his ear, "Don't judge by his appearance. I look on the thoughts and intentions, so listen to me. Next!"

Seven times Jesse parades another son in front of Samuel, and seven times he says "Next!" Finally there are no more sons waiting in the wings. Samuel has a moment of panic. God sent him here, but God doesn't want any of these fine young men?

"Are these all the sons you have?" he asks, trying not to seem worried.

"Well, there's David—he's just a boy. He's out with the sheep."

"Bring that boy to me."

And the rest is history.

What a story to tell our youth! As they search for their significance, as they seek their self-confidence, we can assure them that God recruits everyone into God's kingdom—even small grubby shepherd boys.

affirmations and expressions of love and care may be perceived as hollow and without meaning. If, on the other hand, a person's inner conviction says "I'm okay," then warmth and affirmation from others confirms what the person already knows inside.

Parents play a major role in their son or daughter's self-concept. Setting high expectations can be a good thing, but demanding perfection is setting the teen up for failure. And if the parents don't compliment and affirm the teen for small and large accomplishments, the teen will look elsewhere for the warm fuzzies she needs.

"When I'm not so good in sports, thank you for telling me it was great that I tried, rather than making me practice more," one daughter wrote her parents in a note. "You'll never know how much that meant to me."

Not all teens have parents who can lead and affirm them in positive directions, and when that isn't the case, adult friends for those teens become critical to their development. And, even with positive role modeling from parents and other adults, we know that in the short run peers are often more influential in a teen's search for significance. Young people will work long hours in order to have the car, clothes, cosmetics, or expensive electronic equipment they need to be "in." Some will use alcohol and drugs to shoehorn into a group.

Christina knew she couldn't smoke while she was in America as an exchange student. It was against the organization's rules. But Christina wanted friends in her new high school, and the people she liked smoked. So Christina began smoking with them until the day her host parents confronted her with the fact that she was smelling like smoke. Christina admitted, through tears, that it was her desire to make friends that led her to break the organization's rules. Christina decided that day to base her significance on her relationship with her host family more than on her smoking with friends.

Constructing the Me I Think You See

Cognitive psychology teaches that significant relationships become the "blankies" youth carry with them to mediate their passage from the primary family into the public and sometimes scary world of adulthood. In these relationships, adolescents discover who they are through the eyes of others they trust. Faith development researcher James W. Fowler describes the adolescent thought process in a couplet: *"I see you seeing me; I construct the me I think you see."* Adolescents, particularly, need friendship with an adult who sees in them potential they do not necessarily see in themselves. Studies consistently show that a relationship with such an "adult guarantor" has the most positive influence on overall youth development of all the forms of youth ministry.

And now for the exciting part. We, the church, have the privilege and the responsibility to see our youth with eyes and words that will help them shape their identity as confident children of God. It happened to Mary when the angel Gabriel visited her, and it can happen to our youth today—like the angel's greeting to the adolescent Mary, "Greetings, favored one!" Only the church allows us to see ourselves as God sees us: favored, beloved, blessed.

God's plan for Mary was certainly one-of-a-kind. But God also has plans for each of us, some of which we know and some which remain to be discovered. Part of the "plan" involves helping youth discover their significance, and inviting them into a redeeming relationship with Jesus Christ, a church community, and the world.

Be All That You Can Be

Have you ever gone shopping with a teenager? Have you ever talked to a teen about his "dream car"? Have you ever listened to a girl talk about the boy she'd give anything to have on a date?

Underneath the search for the clothes, car, and guy who are "just right" is the search for significance. And in that search is the desire to be more, have more, live more.

Our Western culture clamors to provide the end of this search. The media bombard us with the notions that sex brings fulfillment, violence solves problems, and winning is everything. Advertisers demonstrate how the right shampoo will get you the guy, the right car will get you the girl, and the right clothes will make you desirable. Politicians promise "the world" to teens at the expense of the rest of the world, and schools push students to compete in order to be deemed "successful." And of course the military promises "Be all that you can be."

Look at these promises from the viewpoint of a teenager. Who wouldn't want sexual fulfillment? Who wouldn't want to win? Who wouldn't want the guy or girl of their dreams? Who wouldn't want to be successful? Who, in the search for self, wouldn't want to be all that he or she can be?

How can the church compete with the millions of dollars spent on such promises? How can we communicate our message with the glitz of the Internet? How can we sell what God has to offer?

We can't.

What we have to offer our youth is a God who loves them unconditionally, a community of faith who will stand by them, and a body of believers who will take interest in each one of them. We offer them significance as favored, beloved, blessed children of God. We offer them our patience. We offer them the opportunity to be all that they can be—loving expressions of God's love in the world.

It's the least—and the most—we can do.

SECTION 2

What Does the Church Have to Offer?

CHAPTER 3

Theological Foundations

THIS BLUEPRINT will focus on four basic beliefs that form the foundation of our youth ministry rebuilding project:

1. God is Creator.
2. God through Christ provides the way of salvation.
3. God is present through the Holy Spirit.
4. God empowers Christians to reveal God's saving purposes to the world.

1. *God is Creator.* We and our youth are created in the image of God. As our Parent, God has invested a lot in us. Something of God's own self has been planted within each of us, and just as earthly parents want to see their children grow and relate to them, so God desires a relationship with us.

God desires our worship and our love. But God's love doesn't stop when we fail to respond. Youth need to hear that. Youth need to know that mistakes and failures do not separate them from the love of God. Adults who work with youth need to remember it. The "unlovely" or inactive or frustrating kids are just as valuable in God's sight as the kids who do everything right. God doesn't create "higher" or "lower" value people. Society does, and we tend to buy into society's evaluations. Kids need to know this, but even more importantly, they need to see it modeled for them. Guess who is called to do the modeling!

Being created in God's image means our lives should reflect God. In Jesus we see God's intention for us: wholeness, justice, peace, and right relationships. The stories of Jesus' time on earth show us how we are to relate to God and to each other.

2. *God through Christ provides the way of salvation.* Youth question and experiment. It's their job. They often know what's right but don't always do it. To know that God is hanging in there with them during their years of uncertainty, and that Jesus offers them forgiveness and new beginnings—that's the good news we share with them.

We need to recognize that this good news comes differently to different people. For the young person who was born into a family active in the community of faith, it may be a recognition and affirmation of what they've learned through their childhood. Hopefully, the young person will say "Yes, I own this for myself. I have grown up with it and I now say yes to following Christ."

The other end of the spectrum may be a "Damascus Road" encounter like the one experienced by the apostle Paul. Salvation may be a decision made out of an intense struggle, resulting in a dramatic, drastic change of life.

However it begins, saying "Yes" to Jesus begins a lifelong transformation of living more and more in the image of God.

3. *God is present through the Holy Spirit.* The Holy Spirit came to believers for the first time at Pentecost, and the Spirit has been blessing and comforting us ever since. This is exciting, reassuring news for youth. The Spirit is with them when they feel alone. The Spirit celebrates with them when they say yes to God. The Spirit calls gifts out of them and empowers them to exercise those gifts as they witness and as they make vocational and relational decisions. The Spirit helps them pray, convicts of sin, and surprises them with connections and "coincidences" that will bring them joy in the knowledge that God really is a part of putting their life blueprint together.

4. *God empowers Christians to reveal God's saving purposes to the world.* The good news of God's salvation in Jesus Christ is for all people. Christ's commission of Matthew 28:18-20 is to "go and make disciples of all nations." The Scriptures expect Christians, as a body (the church), to be a sign of God's reign in the world. When our words coincide with our actions, such a dynamic witness impacts the world. It's characterized by:

• *Holy living.* The Christian life gains credibility when society sees Christians living as a transformed community, obedient to the Scriptures.

God Provides—and How!

Isaac said to his father Abraham, "Father!" And he said, "Here I am, my son." He said, "The fire and the wood are here, but where is the lamb for a burnt offering?" Abraham said, "God himself will provide the lamb for a burnt offering, my son."
(Genesis 22:7-8b)

Imagine being in young Ike's shoes. He's been brought up in a God-fearing, God-loving home. He's heard the story of his miraculous birth. He knows that his life is a great gift from the Creator God to his aged parents.

Now he's on a trip up the mountain to offer a burnt offering to God. He enjoys the trip—the scenery, the fresh air, being with his dad. But he is starting to wonder if his father isn't having a major "senior moment"—like forgetting to take the sacrificial lamb along.

No lamb, no offering, Ike thinks. He hates to challenge his dad, but he decides he'd better ask.

His dad assures him that "God will provide."

Whatever, Ike thinks.

But then things go from weird to horrible, and Ike finds himself on top of the pile of wood, staring at the knife blade in his father's hand. He can't believe it! He can't understand it!

Imagine the rush of relief and thankfulness that flooded Ike's body when the angel called off the killing. Like anyone else with a "near-death" experience, I bet he was praising God long and loud for days to come.

Ike knew God to be his Creator, he knew the need for a sacrificial lamb, and he knew the intimate presence of God in his life. This faith was modeled for him by his parents, and as he grew he came to own it for himself. Today, we model and communicate to our youth that we are created by God, that Jesus is the sacrificial lamb for our salvation, and that God fills us with the intimate presence of the Holy Spirit.

- *Compassion.* This witness of Christian love, commanded by Christ, is a powerful reflection of God's love for the world.
- *Unity.* As Christians function together in unity and love, we reflect the image of God. In a word-weary society, authentic expressions of joy, fellowship, and worship have great impact.
- *Reconciliation and peace.* We witness to God's reign, marked by expressions of peace and justice, when we show reconciling love to a society marked by alienation and violence. Christians need to stand on the side of the disadvantaged and discouraged. Followers of Christ—the Prince of Peace—must also express peace in their world.
- *Sharing our stories.* The Holy Spirit empowers Christians to speak boldly about the good news of Christ (Acts 1:5). All Christians have powerful stories to tell of how Christ forgives sin and gives new purpose and meaning in life. The combined witness of the church, as a body, and individual Christians is what the world needs to hear (2 Corinthians 3:2).

CHAPTER 4

Growing "Flowers of Faith"

THIS BOOK is a blueprint for *congregational* youth ministry because the congregation's business is to provide the environment and support system that enables youth to build their own lives. Here's how congregations can provide such an environment:

Youth Group

In the early part of the 20th century, the setting for young people to learn and socialize within the Mennonite churches was known as a literary society. In the late '40s, a new interest in ministry to youth took hold in the churches, resulting in highly structured denominational, district, and congregational youth group programs. Several decades later, Christian Endeavor, or "C.E.," programs on Sunday evening provided a place for youth to gather and grow spiritually together.

Youth groups have served as a primary connecting point between youth and their congregations for over 50 years, and more and more churches are taking new steps in their approach to youth ministry. While youth groups can still be effective ministry settings, there are several factors that affect their ability to help youth build their lives:

1. *The competition has increased dramatically.* Movies, computers, videos, concerts, cruising, sports, school extracurricular activities, homework—the numbers of things youth cram into their lives these days is huge compared to several decades ago. The result is twofold: youth will not tolerate a boring youth group program, which puts a lot of pressure on the leaders; and youth group just isn't a priority in their schedules like it was in the past.

2. *A few adults are taking most of the responsibility.* As youth get

too busy to put time into youth group, it falls on the adult leaders to maintain a quality program. Some churches employ youth pastors or associate pastors whose portfolio involves working with young people. Others depend on youth sponsors to provide the leadership for the youth group—adults who have jobs, families, and their own long list of commitments.

3. *The youth group becomes a separate "youth congregation" paralleling the life of the congregation.* The sponsors and leaders are viewed as the bridge between the two "congregations," the youth are not active participants in congregational life, and there are few meaningful contacts between youth and adults in their church family.

A Model for Today

The days of youth being set apart from the congregation are over. Today, more and more congregations see themselves as communities of faith that invite all ages to be an integral part of congregational life including worship, fellowship, service, mission, and recreation. Every person is encouraged to come to the church family to help maintain perspective on what's happening in the world, to find renewal in their relationship with God, and to give and receive the support of Christian sisters and brothers.

In a community of faith, people are not seen as objects to be acted upon, but rather as individuals who are actively involved. They are shaping their own life which will in turn shape the life of the community. This "shaping" in a young person's life is described by Michael Warren:

> It is the nature of young people to have to discover their own word
> of faith. The flower of faith cannot be transplanted because it would
> then be one person's flower of faith, growing in another person's soil.
> The flower of faith has to grow from seed in each person's special
> soil and grow as one's own flower.

Congregations that help youth to grow their own special "flowers of faith" will help youth prepare a soil of biblically based values and beliefs. Such a community of faith pays close attention to helping youth develop a sound decision-making process. Although it is deeply interested in the decisions youth make, the congregation asks how it can assist as their identities take shape rather than providing a mold and asking them to step into it.

Active involvement in a congregation is one of the best ways for youth to sketch what will become the blueprint of their lives. The youth of Wilmot Mennonite Church in Ontario know it well. It used to be, the worship band consisted of "three old men with beards and guitars," as described by 19-year-old Andrew Weber. One of the "old men" happened to be his father Bruce. One of the other members, Dave, had a daughter Jenny-Lee who was the same age as Andrew.

"Our pastor (Glyn Jones) wanted youth to be more involved in the service, so we joined our parents in the band," Andrew said. Before long, Andrew's brother Josh and Jenny-Lee's sister Lindsey joined the group. Five more teens became intrigued with the idea and contributed their vocal skills.

So, Wilmot had a youth worship band. But that's not all.

"Sharon Heipel, one of our church accompanists, decided to get children involved in the prelude and postlude," Jenny-Lee remembered. "I'd been playing the piano in church. But then one day someone passed away and none of our adult pianists was available to play for the funeral, so they asked me. I've played for two more since then."

There's more. Jenny-Lee and other youth have been both song and worship leaders for the congregation. "It's a bit nerve-racking the first time," Jenny-Lee said. "I led the songs I knew well and got my sister to accompany me. With the worship leading, we do the call to worship, the Scripture reading, and the opening prayers. Leading the sharing is tough—we don't usually do that."

Mitch, a high school senior from another congregation, had this to say in church the day he graduated: "Soon I'll be leaving this place, but not really. You will go with me. You treated me like a real person. I argued with you, prayed with you, and even preached with you. You helped me when I was hurting, and I believe I helped you when I could see your hurt. I was a teacher . . . and a regular participant in worship. Those were the sharing places that helped me grow."

Atmosphere and Experiences

A blueprint is just blue marks on paper until you buy the lumber and start hammering. A vision statement is just words on paper until

A Flower of Faith

Elizabeth Dirks grew up Catholic. So Catholic, in fact, that she became a nun as a child. By the time she was 12, she was hearing stories of heretics being killed because they didn't believe everything the Catholic Church taught.

A curious and bright young woman, Elizabeth wondered why people were rejecting the teachings of the Roman Catholic Church, so she decided to study the Bible for herself. Her studies led to doubts of her own. She began to ask the other nuns questions they didn't like to be asked. In fact, she stirred up enough trouble, she was imprisoned within the convent for a year on suspicion of heresy.

Some of the nuns felt sorry for her and helped Elizabeth escape, dressed as a milkmaid. She walked to the home of Anabaptists, who took her in and nurtured her growing faith. Soon she was baptized and an active member of the Anabaptist church. She lived with a widow woman, and together they shared their faith with others.

Elizabeth was arrested in 1549 and accused of heresy and of being Menno Simons' wife. At her trial, the council ordered her to give them the names of people she had taught and the person who baptized her. They asked about her beliefs regarding church teachings. Elizabeth remained strong. She told them her beliefs, but she never revealed a name.

Elizabeth was taken to a torture chamber. Thumbscrews were put on her thumbs and forefingers until blood squirted out. Elizabeth prayed.

The executioner put screws in her shins, dislocating her joints. Elizabeth cried out for God's help but would not reveal any names. As a result, she was given the death penalty.

On May 27, Elizabeth Dirks was drowned.

you buy into it with your heart and start acting it out. Two areas in which congregations need to "act out" this vision for youth are atmosphere and experiences.

Atmosphere includes how members live their values, how they express their attitudes, what they demonstrate in their lifestyle. How do youth observe adults relating to each other? How do they feel adults relating to them? How are they included in committees, worship, and all of church life?

Atmosphere is also the facility where youth meet in the church. One rural church has such an inviting atmosphere that its youth rent videos and buy snacks on a Friday night, take them to "their room" at the church, and spend the evening there together.

Another church invites the president of its youth group to be a part of the church council. A congregation in Edmonton, Alberta, hires the young people to provide child care during the congregational meeting, thus "killing three birds with one stone"—solving the child care need, providing interaction between the generations, and helping the youth raise money for their service project or convention trip.

Experiences are times when youth can explore and share about their faith. Experiences are as numerous and varied and creative as the congregation that plans them: service trips, youth Sundays, youth conventions, teaching vacation Bible school, singing in the choir, silent retreats, street witnessing, working on disaster service projects.

The impact of experiences in the spiritual growth of our youth is illustrated by research from the University of Indiana that revealed the following:

After 30 days, students remember:

10% of what they hear
15% of what they see
20% of what they hear and see
40% of what they discuss
80% of what they do
90% of what they teach.

Not only do these statistics show how important it is for youth to be immersed in active experiences in their congregation, but they point out the value of learning as a result of teaching. Many of us who are teachers would be the first to admit that we enjoy teaching because of what we learn in the process. Perhaps one of the greatest unexplored ministries of youth in our congregations is in helping to teach younger children, as well as being responsible for occasionally leading the lesson for their peers.

I've seen the value of youth teachers in several areas in my home congregation, and been amazed at the results. One area is vacation Bible school. It is simply "understood" that our youth will never schedule a service trip during vacation Bible school because they are such an integral part of that week as teachers and recreation leaders. The other instance was when the youth group executive agreed to present the input for one Wednesday evening program. People we would have expected to talk and teach did so. But so did "the quiet guy" who surprised us all. And guess what—their peers gave them the listening respect that we adult sponsors and leaders sometimes have to beg for!

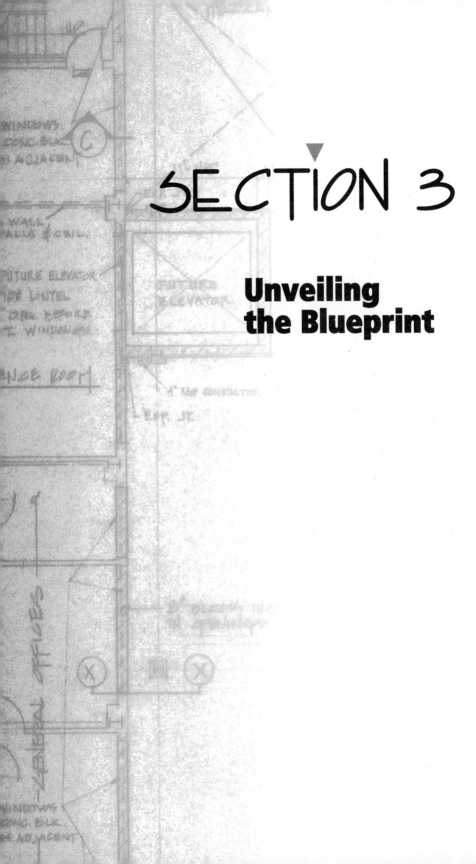

SECTION 3

Unveiling
the Blueprint

CHAPTER 5

A Vision for Youth Ministry

THE MOST IMPORTANT part of developing a blue-print happens before anything is put on paper. The owners of the new or rebuilt structure have a vision for how it's to be used. Remember the old barn? It was the dreams and visions running through our heads that got us excited about its new possibilities. First we had to have a vision, then we could draw a floor plan, and only then could they order the lumber.

The reality for many is that they "order the lumber" and build something without an overall floor plan. I know. I've panicked on Saturday night for coming up with a Sunday school lesson for the next day. I've walked into my conference library and looked for "something, anything" to do in youth group. I've gravitated toward materials that give me activities and quick how-to instructions without making me read a lot of theology or philosophy. I like the smell of new lumber and my busy life only allows enough time to build something that is both quick and, hopefully, effective.

Unfortunately, we've thrown together a shack when we could have built a beautiful home. What's missing is the overall blueprint. A plan for building.

The Importance of a Mission Statement

Imagine that you decide to take a family vacation. Everyone's thrilled. You pack your suitcases, stuff the car, fill it up with gas, and hit the road. After several days of captivating travel games, rousing campfire songs, heartwarming conversation, snacks, naps, and bathroom breaks, someone in the backseat finally asks, "Are we there yet?" Then it hits you. You realize that you never decided on a destination, nor on a way to get there. After a few anxious moments, you shrug your shoulders and chuckle, "Who cares! We're having a blast, aren't we?"

As ridiculous as this story sounds, many youth ministries are in a similar situation—no idea how to get to a place they're not planning to reach. But they're having a great time not getting there.

Having a clear, compelling mission statement answers the question, "Where are we going?" and brings the future into focus.

There is also a unifying quality about a mission statement. When teens, adults, volunteers, and staff move toward a common goal, they find themselves moving closer together.

A good mission statement motivates. It becomes the lifeblood and the driving force behind a ministry. People focus energy on lighting fires, not on putting them out.

Drafting a mission statement provides a youth ministry with an opportunity for evaluation. You have the permission to ask yourselves, "Why are we doing what we're doing?" Down the road, the same mission statement can help you ask "Are we doing what we agreed we'd be doing?"

Key Components of a Mission Statement*

Well-written mission statements should reflect your youth ministry's purpose, values, and strategy.

• *Purpose*—Tells *why* a youth ministry exists and what it hopes to accomplish. In defining purpose, begin with Scripture. Explore key Gospel texts (Matthew 5:13-16; 22:34-40; 28:18-20; Mark 1:15; 8:27-9:1; 12:28-34; Luke 10:25-37; 24:45-49; John 20:21-23) and other significant New Testament passages (Acts 1:8; Romans 1:16-17; 2 Corinthians 5:18-20; Ephesians 3:10-11).

• *Values*—Clarify what is unique about your ministry and what it will emphasize: a commitment to the Scriptures? relevant teaching? radical discipleship? Spiritual life and prayer? missions? contemporary worship?

• *Strategy*—Closely tied to the question, "Where are we going?" is the question, "How are we going to get there?" Frustration grows in a youth ministry that has a clear purpose but no strategy—lofty

---

*This section and next contributed by Wendell Loewen, Bible and religion professor at Tabor College, Hillsboro, Kansas.

goals that are never realized because no one has any idea how to reach them.

Creating a Mission Statement

Perhaps the most effective setting for creating a mission statement is a leadership retreat. Get broad input so there will be wide ownership of the statement. A leadership retreat would include both committed, spiritually mature students, along with parents and adult staff.

Drafting a strong mission statement is no easy task, even in a retreat setting. Here's a place to start:

Leadership Retreat Outline

Session One: What Is Our Purpose? After a time of prayer for the retreat, divide participants into balanced (gender, age) smaller groups. Assign each group two or three New Testament texts that focus on the ministry of Christ's church (passages listed above would be a good start). Ask groups to identify and briefly explain key words found in each text. Compile a list together. Highlight words or ideas that groups hold in common. With these findings try finishing the sentence, "Our purpose is to. . . ." This session will help focus the retreat, and root your mission statement in the biblical purpose of the youth ministry.

Session Two: Where Are We Now? Assess both strengths and weaknesses of your ministry's current situation.

Invite individual participants to answer the following questions:
- What do you think are the strengths of our youth ministry?
- What do you think are the weaknesses of our youth ministry?
- What are your hopes and dreams for the youth ministry?

When everyone has completed the task, form groups and have the individuals compare their answers. Ask each group to report a summary of their discussion. Ask: "What points were similar? What are the most striking differences?"

Session Three: How Are We Going to Get Where We Want to Go? Now that you have a basic understanding of your purpose (where you want to go), and have assessed your current situation (where you are now), you are able to discuss strategy (ways of getting where you want to go).

Reviewing your purpose, strengths, weaknesses, and dreams. Now, in groups, brainstorm at least three strategies that will help accomplish your purpose. Come back together as a group and have one person from each group share the group's suggestions.

Ideas will probably include specific ways to do hand-holding and finger-pointing (see chapter 1) toward Christ (evangelism), building skills for helping youth shape identity and discover significance (see chapter 2), productive ways to build youth in their faith (nurture), and practical strategies to send them into the world (ministry).

Session Four: Creating the Mission Statement. Building on your previous sessions, ask small groups to craft a creative mission statement. Their assignment is to write it in 25 words or less. Now, together as a large group, have one person from each group write down their statement on an overhead, white board, or piece of butcher paper. As the retreat's facilitator, you may have to find inventive ways of incorporating the ideas expressed in each of the statements into one comprehensive (but concise) statement.

The final statement may sound something like this:

> Our mission: to honor our Creator with a ministry that helps youth uncover their life's blueprint, inspires them to follow Jesus, and releases them to minister in the world.

By the end of the retreat there may be some "word-smithing" yet to be done. And the mission statement may spark a more comprehensive document that more fully develops the principles expressed in it.

After the Retreat. Breathe life into your newly formulated mission statement by encouraging youth to write slogans, or compose poems and songs based on the ideas in the mission statement. Create artwork or logos for T-shirts, letterhead, and website design. These activities will help reinforce the ideals reflected in your mission statement and will stimulate imagination to express your ministry's purpose.

Another example of a mission statement is in Appendix A. This is the Congregational Youth Ministry Statement adopted in 1997 by the Mennonite Church and the General Conference Mennonite

Church. Following the statement is an outline that fleshes out specific goals and expectations. You may wish to use that statement as the basis for your own congregational youth ministry, or as a beginning point to form your own.

Lesson from the Goats

Ulrich Zwingli and Martin Luther worked closely in leading the 16th-century Reformation, but they didn't always agree. One time, their conflict was so serious that they resolved to go to separate places to meditate and pray for direction. Zwingli retreated to a hamlet in the Swiss Alps. One day, while contemplating outside the cottage, he noticed two goats on a mountain trail. One goat was going up the mountain, the other was coming down. Ulrich watched with great interest as the goats met and discovered that the road was two narrow for them to pass each other. Zwingli waited for the inevitable fight. He saw them bow their necks as if they were going to ram and butt heads. But then the strangest thing happened. The goat going up the mountain lowered himself to the ground, and allowed the one coming down to gently step over him.

Zwingli said that was the message from the Lord for him that day—that the person who will bend low will be raised high.

This story—and many others—are part of the Anabaptist heritage. Our mission with youth is to tell the stories of our ancestors in the faith, to share our own stories and faith journeys, and to walk with them as they come to know the greatest story ever told.

CHAPTER 6

Construction Details

THE BLUEPRINT is spread out on the table before us. We have dovetailed our knowledge of the milieu in which our youth are growing with the mission for our ministry with them. This blueprint carries tremendous potential, but at this point it's just blue lines on paper. We're eager to order the lumber—the actual building elements of our ministry together. But "everybody knows" we still need to ask: Is the site prepared? Is the weather cooperating? Do we have the necessary equipment lined up? Do we have the carpenters, electricians, and plumbers on board to contribute their skills?

Our model for youth ministry has eight general considerations we need to look at before we pick up the hammer. These may seem obvious, but sometimes the obvious is also the easiest to forget.

1. *Focus on each youth*. Despite our culture's obsession with freedom and individualism, humans are group oriented. We educate in groups according to age. We worship in groups, play in groups, work in groups. Yet who of us hasn't witnessed someone in our youth group being left out because he or she doesn't fit the mold?

The other side of the picture is those youth who stand out from the group because they are highly gifted in music, athletics, leadership, appearance, etc. Sometimes people want to be around them for their own self-gain, not because they care about the person as an individual.

Congregations can be lulled into expecting youth leaders and sponsors to be the primary adults who relate to youth. Likewise, it's easy for sponsors and leaders to focus on those youth who are the most responsible and responsive, and give very little time to the quiet kids on the fringe. One of the most important considerations within a congregation is to determine if and how each young person is receiving ministry from the church.

2. *Youth will be at different points on their faith journey.* Some disrupt Sunday school and drive you crazy with their inattentiveness. Others will be asking for baptism. Some will volunteer to read Scripture in worship, and others won't darken the sanctuary door. Some will invite unchurched youth to your youth group. Others you will secretly wish someone else would invite to their group!

The faith journey for youth (and for all of us) is studded with peaks and valleys. Peak times will embrace new insights and a closeness to God, giving renewed enthusiasm and commitment. But much of our time will be spent in the valley where growth is slower and commitment seems to waver.

Keep in mind the image of the sower, seed and soil. We sow the seeds of faith in the soil of our youth, but it is up to the Spirit to make them grow. We may or may not ever see the harvest, but we still sow with abandon.

3. *Positive relationships are key.* Does each young person have good interaction with others in Sunday school? Does each one feel personally and warmly welcomed by someone in the congregation on Sunday morning? Do the youth who are "successful" get significantly more attention than those who aren't outstanding in something?

In the past, or in today's rural churches, many youth attended both the same church and school. Their friendships and their ability to care for each other was already built in. More recently, youth in the same church don't go to the same schools, or even live in the same community. Their only contact with each other is in church settings. That means they'll need group-building exercises in Sunday school and youth group in order to feel free to share and have fun together.

Likewise, positive intergenerational contacts usually don't just happen. They have to be planned. Whether it's a mentoring program, a game night, or a potluck with "assigned seating," congregations need to provide the settings for youth and adults to relate to each other and to establish the affirming relationships that feel so good for both parties.

4. *Special events equal special opportunities.* A logical way to affirm young people is to recognize their achievements. Some churches talk about them during sharing time, others post clippings on the bulletin board or list them in the newsletter.

Unfortunately, those who cannot make such outstanding achievements never get recognized. Consequently, it is important for congregations to find ways to recognize the uniqueness of each young person. When?

Baptism is the most important time. For some churches it continues to be celebrated in a group—a class studies membership issues and is baptized. Other congregations are planning individual, special services for each young person. The person being baptized helps plan the service, shares his or her understanding of faith and commitment to Christ, and perhaps also shares some music, a reading, artwork, or liturgical dance.

Birthdays are common to everyone, and it's a good time to acknowledge a young person. A phone call, card, small gift, or refreshments are all easy ways to say "You're special! Happy birthday!"

Driver's license. Obtaining a driver's license is a much-anticipated event in most teens' lives. Why not recognize it as a congregation, perhaps with a symbolic key chain and a special prayer for sound judgment and protection while driving?

Graduation from high school is a significant milestone. One congregation presents a special coffee mug to each graduate on Sunday morning, followed by a carry-in meal where each young person shares about their future plans. Other congregations present personalized Bibles to graduates.

Beginning a mentoring relationship is a time for celebration. Congregations often recognize this potentially significant relationship as part of a Sunday morning worship, asking parents of the young person to stand with their son or daughter as a signal of their support for their child and the mentor.

A 12th-birthday celebration is a special rite of passage celebration in some congregations. As the young person approaches this birthday, he or she receives a visit from the pastor or associate pastor. Susan Allison-Jones, associate pastor at Breslau Mennonite Church in Ontario, considers this event to be a highlight for her as well as the young person. "If the child was dedicated in this congregation twelve years ago, we talk about the fact that the same congregation is still here for them, supporting them in their journey. If the child wasn't in our church that long, we say how glad we are to have him or her and their family in our midst. I give them *The Promise Bible*, with highlights of God's promises, and encourage them to ask their parents or us pastors if they have questions. I talk about how I'm eager to get to know them more, and just do what I can to help the congregation and them celebrate this moment in their lives."

When Becky Driedger went through the process, her mother, Jan, said, "It was a very positive experience for us because we were new to the congregation. It introduced us to the church family. Becky sang as part of her sharing, and the congregation hadn't known she could do that. She received a lot of affirmation for singing, and it was a good self-esteem builder. This was also a good opportunity for me as a parent to reflect on her life, and for Nick her stepfather to do something together with her. I've never seen this done before in a church and I think it's a neat idea."

5. *Youth learn through reflecting on their experiences.* Teens, like children, learn best from experience as opposed to simply discussing ideas or concepts. But teens, unlike children, have the capacity to think abstractly and generalize. They can learn from experiences and apply them to other circumstances. So that means it's important to plan special events where youth (and adults as well) get out of their day-to-day rut and experience something different. One congregation plans an annual service experience in Mexico where youth come face-to-face with conditions that often exist in third world countries. Another congregation tries to make a family heritage tour possible for each young person.

Youth don't have to go away to learn from experiences. Some of the most "teachable moments" come out of day-to-day interactions in school, with peers, and in the church family.

The most significant learning from experiences comes through the ability to reflect on and generalize about them. Seeing poverty first-hand offers an excellent opportunity to help young people ask how they might be contributing to those circumstances through their own lifestyles. Going on a tour to see the places important in the heritage of the teen's family could encourage youth to think through their faith and how strong it would be in adverse circumstances.

6. *Listening.* Youth won't be interested in hearing the wisdom we have to impart until we've demonstrated the ability to listen to them. Nonjudgmental listening will get you into their lives quicker than all the right words in the world. You will also find yourself learning from the youth—from their perspectives, from their fresh way of looking at things, from their knowledge of a world that sometimes

Andy Griffith, Luke 6, and Horse Manure

It looked like things were going great with our youth group. Attendance was at an all-time high. They listened to the lessons, laughed with each other, and apparently loved to come to meetings.

But one-on-one, away from church, things weren't always so smooth. Some were picking on others, some were being less-than-Christlike in their attitudes toward each other. Typical teens. Typical human beings.

One evening, we began our session with a segment from the Andy Griffith show that portrayed very clearly the pitfalls of judging people and putting them down. We followed that up with groups presenting skits on Luke 6:37-42, asking them to portray how those verses could be interpreted in a school setting and in a youth group setting. Then it was time for the wrap-up. I summarized what we'd studied, and concluded by saying, "You can come to youth group. You can come to church. You can say you're a Christian. You can read your Bible and pray. But," I paused, placing a newspaper on the floor and turning a garbage bag upside down on the newspaper. The girls nearest the bag gasped as dried horse manure spilled onto the paper in front of them. "But all of that isn't worth any more than the pile in front of you if you can't learn how to treat each other with respect and kindness."

You could have heard a pin drop, or a piece of manure roll.

It goes without saying: All of the programming and all of the blueprints for youth ministry in the world aren't worth more than that pile if we aren't, first and foremost, "incarnating" Christ's love over and over and over.

seems to be changing faster than we adults can keep up. Listen. Then choose your words carefully when they listen to you in return.

7. *Mentoring future leaders.* Part of our role in youth ministry is recognizing, supporting, and encouraging youth with leadership abilities. Sometimes those abilities are obvious, and other times it takes some time for them to emerge. One of the greatest challenges for youth sponsors is to know how and when to give youth responsibility and let them fail, if it comes to that, rather than stepping in to "rescue" them. Youth will learn much more if sponsors help them pick up the pieces, reflect on the experience, and think through how things might be handled differently in the future. Find ways to "set them up for success." Provide just enough guidance that, along with their natural skills and abilities, they will be successful in what they are doing (reading Scripture, playing special music, crafting a Youth Sunday, etc.). Then sit back while they receive the affirmation of the congregation.

8. *Every time there is interaction, there is youth ministry.* We are so accustomed to thinking that youth ministry happens mainly in youth group or Sunday school, but the chance encounter on the street, attendance at their school events, a note in the mailbox, a smile while walking into church on Sunday morning—those mean more to our youth than we know. Youth ministry is people first, and program second.

CHAPTER 7

Bring On the Lumber

WE CONCLUDED the last chapter stating that "every time there is interaction, there is youth ministry." We will now break that umbrella statement down into eleven significant settings where congregations can open the potential for youth ministry to happen. These settings are our lumber—they are the framework of our youth ministry activity. These "rooms" are what turn our blueprint into a building, our ideas into action. They are:

1. Congregational worship
2. Sunday school
3. Youth group
4. Instruction for baptism and church membership
5. Mentoring relationships
6. Peer ministries
7. Family life
8. Camps
9. Conventions
10. Service and mission experiences
11. Spiritual practices

Just as each room in a newly built house has its own attraction and function, so each of these settings plays a different role in a young person's faith journey. The most rewarding and effective approach is to see them as one larger, coordinated effort. Let's take a look at each setting or "room."

Setting 1: Congregational Worship

The midsized church in central Kansas had recently welcomed a new, energetic pastor. One morning, on his way to Sunday school after the worship service, one of the youth commented to his teacher: "I'm having trouble getting my nap in church with Corey preaching."

Oh, to have that dilemma in all congregations! Fact is, some youth are in worship services because their parents make them come. Some are there out of habit. Some are there because they enjoy the music. And some are there because they truly enjoy worshiping God with their church family.

Congregational worship is a very important setting, and in some cases the only contact a young person will have with the church. Unfortunately, the reality is that congregational worship varies in its appeal to youth as well as to adults. The difference is that adults are more likely to keep coming out of habit and compromise on what is "meaningful" to them in order to be a part of corporate worship. For youth, if it isn't meaningful to them, they will be out of there at the first opportunity.

So what should a congregation do? Cater entirely to the wishes of the under-18ers? Not at all. But if congregations seek ways to be more "youth friendly" and to impact their lives in this setting, adults may also respond positively. How?

Appeal to all five senses, different learning styles, both intellect and feeling. The possibilities are endless when we realize that we can use different approaches to worship and to communicating God's word. Music is an obvious variable—and many congregations are enjoying a balance between hymns and contemporary praise songs. Scripture is being shared interactively—when the story of the feeding of the 5,000 was told in one service, everyone received bread and butter sandwiches. Shana Peachey Boshart recalls how West Union Mennonite Church in Parnell, Iowa, experienced the same story:

"Martha Yoder started with the assumption that five loaves and two fish were meant to be the boy's lunch, the amount needed for one person. She decided that seven kernels of popcorn would represent one meal. Seven times 5,000 people would be 35,000 kernels of popcorn needed to represent the amount of food Jesus' miracle produced. She counted the number of kernels in a quarter cup and using that figure, came up with how many quarter cups were needed for 35,000 kernels. Then she popped that much popcorn.

"When she told the story in church, she first held up a really small plastic bag with seven pieces of popped popcorn in it, representing the five loaves and two fish—lunch for one person. Then she told us how she popped enough to represent the feeding of the 5,000, and asked the children in the room how many bags of popcorn they thought it made. She started pulling two-gallon plastic bags of popcorn out from where they had been hidden. The whole congregation was riveted, watching her pull out bag after bag. The visual contrast between the tiny bag of seven kernels and the 21 (yes, 21!) large bags was startling. We saw with our own eyes just a hint of the magnitude of that miracle."

When congregations worship together in creative ways, it won't be just the youth who will have "trouble taking a nap" during the service.

Involve youth in the worship services and on the worship planning committee. Remember the youth at Wilmot Mennonite Church who were in the worship band, led congregational music and worship, and played the piano? Remember my mini-lecture about setting them up for success? Now do it. Invite youth to be a part of all aspects of your worship. And if they aren't perfect, it's okay! Isn't it better to have churches growing because "imperfect youth" are filling the pews than churches dying because "perfect adults" are getting older?

Sermons for everyone. A sermon is not the time for a theological discourse. It is a time to communicate God's message in a way that connects with most of the listeners, including junior high and senior high youth.

One way to encourage pastors to prepare sermons that will have meaning for youth is to schedule a "sermon discussion" in Sunday school. Obviously this works best in congregations where Sunday school follows the sermon, but the topic could be talked about in Sunday school prior to the sermon as well. The success of this class will depend on the teacher's ability to get the sermon topic ahead of time and prepare a lesson based on it, but when done right, it is an excellent method of encouraging youth to listen to the sermon.

Youth Sunday. Every Sunday worship should be attractive to youth, but congregations may want to occasionally schedule a Sunday when the speaker, music, and other activities are geared specifically toward the youth. Another take on this is a Sunday worship that is planned entirely by the youth.

One church with the tradition of annual youth-led worship services has appreciated the way the gifts of the youth have been highlighted on that Sunday. Some years, drama is the dominant feature of the service. Other years, the group seems especially gifted in music. One unforgettable service included a youth member sharing her gift of dance as she performed part of the popular Celtic musical "Lord of the Dance."

At least three valuable things happen when youth are asked to lead a worship service.

1. They have to learn before they can share. If their theme is going to be prayer, they will need to study prayer before they can lead others in worship on it.

2. They will take leadership roles. It's youth Sunday, so everyone has to do something. For some, new gifts will come out at this time.

3. They receive affirmation from the congregation.

Setting 2: Sunday School

The Sunday school curriculum at Tabor Mennonite Church included giving the class of junior high boys some homework to bring back the next Sunday. Homework? Junior high boys? In Sunday school? Certainly a recipe for failure.

Surprise, surprise, surprise. Not only did they do the homework one week, but for four consecutive weeks during the Advent season. Why?

They were good kids, sure. And something more. The lessons engaged them in both the biblical story and in what was happening in their lives. They wanted to participate in class, and they were motivated to work outside of class as well.

Sunday school is a struggle in some congregations, with attendance being low or very sporadic. Ideally, Sunday school brings youth of the congregation together for a prime teaching opportunity. For some congregations, Sunday school is the only time all the youth are together, and it doubles as a youth group setting. In those cases, Sunday school time consists of group building activities, youth group business, and some time for teaching. For other congregations where the youth group meets separately, the Sunday school time can be dedicated to Christian education.

Whether the teacher has 20 minutes or an hour, the key to making

Sunday school attractive and effective is to engage the youth. Good curriculum helps a lot. But the bottom line is that curriculum doesn't teach, people do.

Look for curriculum—or create your own lessons—that follow this simple format: LIFE/BIBLE/LIFE. Begin with an activity or question that *draws attention* to an issue youth experience in life right now—make sure the question has a direct tie-in with the lesson to be presented. Help youth express their experience of this issue. Then ask what the Bible says about the issue. Move on to explore what the Bible passage *means* for contemporary life. Finally, get people to respond. Why does the Bible passage *matter*?

What you do in Sunday school should include telling of the biblical story, with special emphasis on the life of Jesus through the study of the Gospels. Youth should be coming to an understanding of God's involvement with humanity through the centuries, of Jesus' life and death and resurrection, and of the establishment of the early church.

"When we tell the whole story of God's interaction with people, it forces us to consider a new worldview in which Christ is at the center," says Gareth Brandt, professor of youth ministry at Columbia Bible College. "Young people will find themselves in the stories. Weaving our own stories with the stories of Scripture is the most relevant way to engage our youth."

Sunday school does not have to be boring. It shouldn't be! The telling of the biblical story along with the stories of our lives invites the involvement of our youth, and leads to the kind of response shown by the junior high boys at Tabor Church.

If youth in your congregation don't hear the biblical story and receive a Christian education in Sunday school, where will they get it? If your youth spend most of their Sunday school time talking about youth group fundraisers, when will they learn about God? Don't get so busy *doing* things with youth that you lose sight of your mission.

Setting 3: Youth Group

Recently, eight young people were baptized into Hoffnungsau Mennonite Church in central Kansas. What was unusual about this baptism in a rural congregation was that five of those eight youth did not come from families active in that church. The parents of one of the girls weren't even at the service.

You know who brought those youth to church? The youth group. This tight-knit group of teenagers hasn't had any formal training in evangelism. They don't have specific goals to "bring kids to the Lord." But God is using them in powerful ways in their schools, communities, and church.

The youth of Hoffnungsau have a strong sense of identity, but it does not represent a barrier between them and the congregation. As mentioned earlier in this book, the goal of a youth group is not to separate the teenagers from the rest of the congregation into their own little "mini-church." Rather, it is a comfortable setting in which they can relate to peers and from which they connect with the congregation in a variety of ways.

Not all congregations will have a "Hoffnungsau" kind of group, and groups may vary dramatically from year to year. Size of church, numbers of young people, commitment, location, and leadership all affect if and what kind of youth group will exist within a congregation. Some congregations struggle to keep something going for five youth, while others hire a youth pastor to oversee more than fifty. Some groups meet every Wednesday night for serious input. Others meet several times a month for fun and fellowship. Some youth groups include grades 7-12, and others have separate groups for 7-8 and 9-12.

Whether your group is 5 or 50, keep in mind:

1. *Acceptance and affirmation* should be priority number one. In building the group identity, stress cooperation, avoid competition, and plan activities such as weekend retreats that help the youth get to know each other. When cliques form, allow them time to be together but also set up other times when you mix the kids up.

2. *Have fun together.* Game nights, progressive meals, video scavenger hunts—be creative and have a good time together.

3. *Get serious together.* Discuss current issues. Talk about God. Pray together. Cry together. Create a safe place for youth to be themselves and to share without being afraid of what someone will say.

4. *Do service and mission ministries.* Whether playing games with residents in the local nursing home or taking a trip across country to clean up with a disaster service project, whether planning a cultural exchange with another youth group or fixing up houses in an urban setting, youth should learn that service opportunities will do more for them than for the people they are "ministering to."

5. *Interact with your congregation and other youth groups.* Plan fun nights and invite your congregation. Do something with a neighboring youth group. Reach out!

6. *Invite sponsors to see this as a longer rather than short-term calling.* Watch the progression in a young person's life from grade 9 to grade 12. Become comfortable praying with a group. Know how to shut the kids up! Know that Youth Sunday will all come together despite how awful it went at "dress rehearsal."

All of these and many more aspects of being a youth sponsor come with time. Acknowledging that family and time commitments do often call sponsors away from youth group, congregations should find ways to encourage and support youth sponsors not to view their term as "two years and then I'm done." Youth who've gotten accustomed to quick turnover of sponsors and leaders are amazed when someone sticks with them longer. Consider your role a call from God not unlike that of a deacon in your church. Your consistent presence in the lives of the youth year after year is a gift God may be calling you to share.

Setting 4: Instruction for Baptism and Church Membership

Baptism, as understood by Anabaptist congregations, is a symbol of a person's decision to follow Christ and unite formally with the church in membership. This milestone event is usually preceded by formal preparation and instruction. In some congregations this is referred to as catechism. Others call it instruction class or Faith Exploration.

Just as the title varies among congregations, the patterns for who takes the class and what is taught differ as well. In some churches, all youth entering a designated grade, such as grade 9, enter the class and study together. Others work as individuals. Whether or not the young person takes the instruction class with a group or on his or her own, it is important that he or she has a choice regarding if and when to be baptized.

The content of the instruction class is usually up to the pastor(s), who teaches the class. One of the reasons some congregations use the title Faith Exploration is to let the youth know that this is a time for them to raise questions about faith, God, Anabaptist beliefs, etc. The class should be a safe place for youth to raise doubts and questions without receiving critical and judgmental response from the pastor. This is a time for youth to ask, learn, and decide if and when they want to be a part of an outward symbol of an inward commitment to Christ and the church.

Some of the areas covered in a Faith Exploration class should include:

- The telling of the biblical story—God's involvement with humanity, Jesus' life and death and resurrection, the early church.
- Reflection on how their faith has developed, including the role of family and congregation.
- The meaning of being a Christian in today's world and what it means to take faith seriously in everyday living.
- The meaning of baptism in the Anabaptist/believers church tradition.
- The place of the Bible in a Christian's experience and the role of other disciplines that shape the Christian life.
- The meaning of church membership, both historically and in the local congregation, including expectations and responsibilities of members.
- The vision and mission of the local congregation, its structure and organization, how it functions.
- Discussion of what it means to be Mennonite/Church of the Brethren, including those beliefs and doctrines held in common and those different from other Christians.
- Specific planning of the baptismal service.

As youth go through their Faith Exploration classes, it is helpful for an adult (mentor, friend, someone trained in spiritual direction) to be available to discuss with them what they are learning, asking, thinking.

Setting 5: Mentoring Relationships

The 9-year-old boy's father and mother were recently divorced. He was having trouble in school. His mother was concerned about him. Then someone came along and became his friend.

Twenty years later, the soap opera in that boy's family had exploded. There were marriages, divorces, extramarital affairs, children out of wedlock, newly discovered half sisters.

And the boy? A wonderful husband to a Christian woman and father to two children, and the teacher/principal of a one-room Christian school in Nebraska.

Several things came together rather than flying apart in that 9-year-old boy's life—a dedicated Christian mother, stepfather, and grandparents. And a special friend—an adult mentor.

One of the most significant connections we can make in youth

"Go Make Disciples"

Now the eleven disciples went to Galilee, to the mountain to which Jesus had directed them. When they saw him, they worshiped him; but some doubted. And Jesus came and said to them, "All authority in heaven and on earth has been given to me. Go therefore and make disciples of all nations, baptizing them in the name of the Father and of the Son and of the Holy Spirit, and teaching them to obey everything that I have commanded you. And remember, I am with you always, to the end of the age." (Matthew 28:16-20)

Eleven people—just eleven people—have been told to make disciples of all nations. Can you imagine?

No media blitz, no Internet, no news or talk shows, no air travel. Nothing is available that would enable them to get the gospel out to all nations. All they have is hearts on fire for a Lord who has changed their lives, and a Holy Spirit ready and willing to help.

It's all they need.

Eleven settings are presented in this chapter—eleven settings where the Holy Spirit can use us to make disciples. We have the media, Internet, television, air travel, and a host of other means to get our message out. But it all still starts in hearts on fire for a Lord who has changed our lives. And it's all still the work of the Holy Spirit.

ministry is a mentoring relationship. This intentional pairing of an adult and youth, usually of the same gender, provides the young person with an adult other than parents to trust, talk to, spend time with, and discuss life concerns. This adult mentor can provide the open, supportive, unconditionally accepting relationship that is so critical to youth as they sort through the decisions of their teen years. Some congregations start the mentoring program with young persons in grade 7; others wait until grade 9. The goal is for the pair to stay together through high school.

Most congregations make the matches by asking the youth who they would like to have as their mentor. Youth may have several suggestions—those persons are approached in order of the youth's preference. The honor of being asked to be someone's mentor is usually all it takes for an adult to say yes.

Once matched, the pair is encouraged to do something together at least once a month, checking in with each other informally in between. The most important task for the mentor is to listen and to help the youth reflect and work through whatever is concerning him or her at the time. This "listening ear" doesn't have to occur in a serious, "tell-me-all-your-problems" setting. Having fun together is a big part of a mentoring relationship.

In addition to listening, a mentor has another very significant task, and that is to remain committed. Those who say they will be a mentor but then don't follow through will do a great disservice to the young person. On the other hand, those who give of themselves in an intentional, committed relationship will contribute immensely to the building of a solid young person. Just ask that teacher in Nebraska.

Setting 6: Peer Ministry

A second one-on-one relationship in our list of settings is Peer Ministry or Peer Helping. This setting helps youth develop special skills so they can reach out and help their peers beyond what a close friendship can do. This approach has been pioneered by Dr. Barbara Varenhorst, a school psychologist in the public school system in Palo Alto, California.

Peer helping consists of three components. Youth enter a period of *training*, after which they may enter into a *peer ministry assignment*.

The final component is an arrangement of *support* during their assignment. Youth who want to become involved must be committed to a time of serious training in building relationship skills. The three components in a little more detail:

Training. Focuses on skills like meeting and communicating with new people, formulating questions that require responses beyond yes or no. The goal is to enable them to form special caring relationships. Those who complete this part of the program will almost always experience significant personal growth. Whether or not they are ready for a peer-helper assignment will be decided in dialogue with the program coordinator.

Ministry involvement. One of the key tasks of the coordinator is to find places where those trained in peer ministry can use their gifts. A logical application for the training would be inviting other youth into the congregation and to youth group, making sure they had a ride to those functions, and taking a special interest in the newcomers. Other peer-helper assignments might include high school youth helping a teacher in a younger Sunday school class, or perhaps begin a special relationship with a resident in a nursing home.

Support. Ongoing support is an important part of this program, so the peer-helper has a place to bring concerns, frustrations, and celebrations. At a minimum, there should be a monthly meeting of all those having assignments.

Some youth are ready for the kind of commitment this setting demands, others don't have the discipline for such involvement. As in mentoring, those who make a commitment to walk with another person but fail to follow through can do a great deal of harm, while those who take it to heart can help change lives.

Setting 7: Family Life

Family life has a significant impact on the attitude of a young person in all areas of life, including how they feel about faith and church.

Teen-parent retreat. A daylong or weekend retreat for parents and teens would have fun elements like the "Parent/Teen Game" (a take-off on the old Newlywed Game television show); as well as input and discussion on issues such as communication, sexuality, peer pressure, etc.

Sunday school electives. Classes on parenting and how to relate to teens could be offered as options for adults in Sunday school.

Including teens in small groups. If parents are in a small group, involve the teens now and then. Focus on topics that are good for teens and parents to discuss together.

Pay attention to mealtime rituals. Compile a pamphlet describing ideas (glean them from actual practices of families in your congregation) for table graces and family time around a meal. Distribute to families with teens in your congregation.

Tough questions. Offer a set of questions that mentors and families could use at home, or on trips with teens, ones like Faith Talk cards, or from *The Book of Questions*—questions that start people off on a hypothetical vein that can lead to meaningful interaction.

Encourage marriage enrichment programs. Healthy marriages contribute to happy teens, as well as showcase skills for future teen relationships. Help parents become involved in at least one marriage enrichment experience during the teen years of their children.

Parent support groups. Sometimes parents just need to talk with other parents where they can be accepted no matter how they think they may have failed. Help provide that kind of setting.

Professional counseling. When families need counseling, encourage it. Help them to get beyond any lingering stigmas. Reassure them that it's better to go for counseling than to pretend nothing is wrong, and possibly lose their family life.

Setting 8: Camps

Many young people point to their camp experience as a spiritual high. Keep this in mind as you build your plan for youth ministry. Camps provide many clear, powerful opportunities for growth in a young person's life. New learning in a natural environment, friendships that may last for years, and independence from parents are all part of the camp experience. To be on the "receiving end" of the camp program can be a moving experience, but to be a part of the program efforts in a leadership role is even more significant. When young people serve as camp counselors and staff members, they gain valuable insights into relationships, planning activities, and the connection between their individual spirituality and the body of believers.

"I was nurtured in faith both in my church and my family," writes

Jeremy Bergen of Winnipeg, Manitoba. "But it was through my experiences at camp that I found myself taking an ownership of my faith that I had not experienced before. As a 16-year-old counselor, cabin devotions were probably the first time I shared my faith publicly. I know with some confidence that having the opportunity of giving leadership at camp confirmed me in my own faith and contributed to making the step of baptism and church membership."

Setting 9: Conventions/Conferences

One of the most rewarding aspects of conventions and conferences is that they bring youth together from all over Canada and the United States, from urban and rural settings, different ethnic groups and cultures. Youth see that they are part of a much larger Mennonite or Brethren body. Their interaction with other youth enlarges their "church family" beyond what they knew in their home community.

While the social life is a highlight for youth at conventions, the number one goal for youth conventions is to call young people to follow Jesus' way. Many congregations assist their youth in raising the money to attend these events, believing it to be a very worthwhile investment that will pay spiritual dividends in the present as well as the future. The letters that arrive in the Mennonite Youth Convention office following a youth convention give unquestionable testimony to the value of this investment.

"Our youth group consists of some churched youth but mainly youth who come on their own from the community," a youth director wrote. "One of the (boys) is 15 years old and comes from a very difficult home life. On the outside he is one of the most obnoxious youth we have—always ready to put someone else down. The night Tony Campolo was calling youth to come forward and surrender to a life of service for Christ, most of my youth went forward, but to my surprise I saw Jonathan up front, he was kneeling and had his face to the ground sobbing. The greatest thing about it too was that our youth were surrounding him and just being there for him. It was at that moment that I knew our youth group would never be the same."

Another young person writes: "Though it was not at a convention that I first dedicated my life to Christ, each one has been a vital stepping-stone in my journey and a time when I have been renewed, inspired, and jolted back into the reality of what it means to follow Jesus."

Other significant outcomes of a convention are mentioned in this letter from a pastor after the youth of his church attended Orlando 97: "A group of our youth was very instrumental in getting a music team going to help lead us (the congregation) in worship. The youth have by themselves begun a teen Bible study they're leading. And largely due to Orlando 97, there is a lot of interest in service and service trips."

"We work to get youth to conference, hoping they will develop a loyalty and affection for conference," says Shana Peachey Boshart, Iowa-Nebraska Conference youth minister. "Our hope is that some-day they will be delegates and want to go [to conference] as adults."

Setting 10: Service and Mission Experiences

What does it mean to "empower youth to bring healing and hope to the world"? It means guiding them in their journey of feeling whole and hopeful within themselves. It means providing settings for them to interact with new people, cultures, economic situations, and ethnic backgrounds, and encouraging them to both give and receive in those settings. It means a New York City youth putting on the "chore boots" of an Iowa farm teen, and a girl from the plains of Saskatchewan riding the subway with her peers in Toronto. It means an exchange of ideas and lifestyles that will increase our global awareness and our ability to bring healing and hope to each other.

Service and mission experiences are evangelism events. Evangelism is sharing God's good news through who we are, what we do, and what we say. It is not something that we "do" to others. Evangelism takes into account that we have much to learn from our hosts even as we receive and share God's love with them.

Young people have many options in which they can explore the two-way experience of service and mission—through youth conventions, service trips, and community involvement. One youth group's service and mission experiences have included buying gas for customers at the local service station, visiting the residents in the local nursing home, and participating in a cultural exchange with a group of Hispanic youth from another part of the country.

Several years ago, Canadian Mennonite Brethren youth attended a youth convention in Winnipeg. This gathering featured big-name speakers, exciting outings, a waterpark, and an "urban plunge" where youth were asked to interview street people on faith issues and serve in a soup kitchen. When evaluations were turned in after the convention, organizers were surprised to see that the urban plunge scored higher than the expensive speakers and entertainment. Giving youth a chance to bring healing and hope to the world is one of the most important ministries we have with young people.

Setting 11: Spiritual Practices

Perhaps we're finally admitting that life is too fast and technology too overwhelming. Or perhaps it just took us a long time to discover what monks have known for centuries. Whatever the reason, practicing spiritual disciplines has resurfaced recently, and youth as well as adults are appreciating these ancient methods of connecting with God and their own spirituality. The practices of silence, meditation, fasting, prayer, and working with a spiritual director are avenues for youth to explore a deeper relationship with God.

Mark Yaconelli, director of the Youth Ministry and Spirituality Project at San Francisco Theological Seminary, has implemented a contemplative approach to youth ministry at Sleepy Hollow Presbyterian Church in San Anselmo, California. He writes:

> Each week at youth group, young people and adults together engage in various spiritual practices. For example, during this past Lenten season groups of adults and youth committed themselves to practicing and sharing different forms of spiritual examination. One group fasted on Thursdays, members of another group engaged in the Ignatian awareness examen over the phone, another group committed itself to intercessory prayer, and members of a fourth wrote letters of gratitude each day. Our hope is that we are offering young people a variety of spiritual practices and intergenerational relationships that will sustain their faith into adulthood and give them a place from which they can counter the destructive forces of our culture.

Deborah Arca, who works with Mark Yaconelli as project manager for YMSP, wrote about another congregation, Westminster Presbyterian Church in Eugene, Oregon, that has seen exciting spiritual growth among its youth.

In this congregation, the youth director has a team of 18 lay volunteers (split between the senior high and middle school youth groups), who meet together regularly to pray for the youth as well as engage in spiritual exercises that help nurture and sustain their own spiritual lives and foster an "alive" spiritual community around the youth group.

As a result of learning and practicing spiritual exercises in their youth group and at a YMSP Spiritual Formation Retreat, youth in this congregation have become more actively interested in serving the church and sharing a new sense of God's presence in their lives by teaching Sunday school and leading worship. Specifically, the youth started a twice-a-week morning prayer service at the church before school, leading meditative singing and the ancient prayer practice "lectio divina." These new midweek morning prayer services, led by the youth, are open to all members of the congregation.

Commenting on the new emphasis in the young people on creating "sacred space" and "sacred time" with others, the WPC youth pastor reflected that "in the midst of their busy and often stressful lives, the youth just enjoy the silence, the solitude, and the space to simply 'be' in the presence of one another and God."

Our Lilly Foundation evaluator for this project visited WPC and reported that the WPC program "has seen a significant increase in numbers attending youth group and a tangible deepening of the spiritual lives of its members."

Setting It Up

It would be a rare congregation that would have strong programs in all eleven of these settings. More likely, congregations will have a strong emphasis on some and little or no activity in others. What's important is that a congregation evaluates the needs of its youth and provides a number of settings where those needs can be met. Getting one program going well and then adding another setting is much better than tackling the whole list at once.

The Youth Ministry Team

THE 1988 EDITION of *Blueprint for Congregational Youth Ministry*, which this book is based on, spoke of a "ministry team whose purpose it will be to develop, oversee, and carry out the total ongoing youth ministry of the congregation." The team would be made up of the following:

• Pastor, or associate pastor with responsibilities for the youth program
• Elder or deacon, representing the congregation's board of elders or deacons
• Two parents of teens
• Two youth who are leaders
• Youth group sponsors
• Mentor program coordinator
• Peer-helper program coordinator
• Family Life program coordinator
• Youth Sunday school superintendent

More than a decade later, this model for a youth ministry team is still working in some congregations. (A more detailed description of this approach is in Appendix B.) However, other congregations that found it too large and cumbersome have modified it to fit their own needs. One such paradigm has been developed by Jonathan Neufeld, Associate Pastor of Bethel Mennonite Church in Winnipeg, Manitoba, and Doug Klassen, pastor of Foothills Mennonite Church, in Calgary, Alberta. Adapted from a course taught by Roland D. Martinson of Luther Seminary, their model consists of three elements:

1. A Youth and Young Adult Initiative Team, consisting of three people and the associate pastor of youth, who "set the congrega-

tion's direction for youth and young adult ministry: identifying purpose and mission, formulating policy and discerning leadership."

2. Impulse Centers—program or task committees that carry out the hands-on work of youth and young adult ministry. Ongoing ministry is accomplished by youth and adults with particular gifts and a variety of responsibilities throughout the congregation. These centers and the people associated with them become as numerous as is needed to carry out the congregation's youth and young adult ministry activities.

3. Youth and Young Adults: Ministry that Matters—an annual gathering during which ministry workers can be nurtured through worship, inspired through prayer, and encouraged through sharing; providing the context in which ministry leaders can be a nurturing community. (For more details on this model, see Appendix C.)

Another approach—one that has grown out of Mark Yaconneli's

A Meeting with Jesus

I'm wondering what a planning meeting was like with Jesus and his disciples.

Did they set goals for the next day or week? Did they know where they would be for the next day's meals? Did they know where they would sleep? Did they check the weather before they made plans to travel? (Red sky at night. . . .) Did they discuss the opposition they would encounter?

Did they talk about the events of the day? Of course. Did they ask questions and get tired of parable answers? Surely. Did they tell jokes? Naturally. Did they take time to pray alone? Without a doubt. Did they pray together? Necessary. Did they grumble? Oh yes. Did they get along with each other? Not always. Did they cry together? At least once. Did they understand who it was that they were following? To a point.

Did they realize that God—the Creator God of the universe—was sitting there beside the fire, roasting a fish, and smiling at them?

Do we?

work in the Youth Ministry and Spirituality Project—invites youth, adult leaders, and congregations to begin developing practices and sensibilities for discerning the presence of God. "As a veteran youth minister in a small suburban church, this model has caused me to shift my priorities from designing entertaining programs to following God's guidance in prayer," Yaconelli writes. "In this approach, youth ministry no longer centers around peppy leaders and programming committees but is focused on adults and young people persistently listening for the movement of God in their lives."

Yaconelli continues: "Our team meetings have allowed the volunteers and myself to continue to serve in youth ministry with a sense of joy and expectation. We leave youth meetings encouraged and renewed rather than burned out. We look forward to our leadership gatherings rather than look for excuses to get out of another boring committee meeting. Most importantly, we are living out the Christian life in a way that is real and visible to young people. We no longer speak to youth of the importance of the Christian faith without experiencing its wonder and power. Seeking the movement of God, we are eager to invite youth to join us in listening for that still small voice that calls out 'I have come that you may have life, and have it abundantly.' " (For more details on this model, see Appendix D.)

The Barn Revisited

REMEMBER the old barn? Come with me now to a farmyard in central Kansas on a clear quiet night in mid-December.

You approach the farm along a sand road, and turn into a lane where a kerosene lantern and several teenage boys are waiting to greet you. "If you have anyone in your car who has trouble walking, you can drive onto the yard," one of them says. "Otherwise, please park in this field."

You park the car in a row of other cars, step out, and walk along a tree-lined lane toward a bonfire in the middle of the farmyard. There you join a group of people standing around the bonfire, softly singing Christmas carols, accompanied by two young men with guitars. A full moon is slowly rising over the large white barn behind the campfire. The evening is perfectly still.

Before long, two teenage girls dressed like angels invite the group around the fire to follow them. You walk down a luminary-lit path along the side of the barn, and approach it from the back side. You pause, sensing something, and then smile as you notice the small herd of sheep and a large white llama, peacefully chewing their cuds and watching as you pass by.

You enter the barn. It's not well-lit, but light enough. Light enough to see a big Holstein cow and her calf in a wooden stall near the door. Light enough to watch an assortment of chickens, ducks, goats, peacocks, and two llamas rustling in the straw in the next stall. And light enough to see what is happening in the open area in the middle of the barn. There, against a backdrop of straw bales, is a living nativity—teenagers portraying Mary and Joseph, a lifelike doll baby, and a much-used real manger. Around them are gathered several more youth and youth sponsors, a baaing sheep, and a friendly dog.

One of the young people reads the Luke 2 account. The youth lead the group in several Christmas carols. The sheep talks during "Silent Night," the cow moos as if on cue in "Away in a Manger," and a donkey leans over its fence and nuzzles your shoulder. You feel the Christmas story as you've never felt it before, and you worship.

Same Structure, New Version

The farmer who built that barn never dreamed people would be worshiping in it. Barns were for animals, grain, and hay, after all. Church buildings were for worship.

Times change, and so do dreams and visions. The structure of the barn remains, the basic structure of our congregations remain. *But what we are doing inside those structures has changed.* It must, if we are going to keep the barn—and the congregation—vibrant with life.

This blueprint for youth ministry is just a blueprint—one that you can build from, change, rearrange to fit your congregation. Take it. Make it work for you. Get to know the youthful lives inside your church family. Wrap them in the warm arms of congregational care, invite them to commitment, and empower them to bring hope to the world.

What a calling! What an awesome privilege.

Congregational Youth Ministry Statement

adopted in 1997 by the Mennonite Church and the General Conference Mennonite Church

THE MISSION *in Mennonite youth ministry is to actively invite every youth to commit to a personal relationship and everlasting adventure with Jesus Christ, mentoring them towards wholeness within a supportive church community, and empowering them to bring healing and hope to the world.*

This mission statement grows out of and embraces the long-term vision statement adopted by the Mennonites in 1995 called *Vision: Healing and Hope*. In addition, the statement has been expanded to name specific avenues in which congregations are encouraged to carry out the mission, and goals have been set to help "measure" the process.

Vision: Healing and Hope

God calls us to be followers of Jesus Christ and, by the power of the Holy Spirit, to grow as communities of grace, joy and peace, so that God's healing and hope flow through us to the world.

1. To follow Jesus Christ more faithfully, we are called to mentor youth to love God with all their heart, soul, mind and strength.

As we:
• enrich our prayer, worship, and study of Scriptures
• offer all that we are and have to God

By:

a. providing an environment where commitment to Christ is encouraged

b. nurturing spiritual disciplines such as prayer, Scripture reading, regular devotions, solitude, reflection and fasting

   c. discipling through biblical teaching

   d. encouraging healthy self-esteem and respect for one's body as the temple of God

   e. modeling biblical stewardship in all areas of life

   f. advocating love, peace, justice as the Christian way of life

   g. guiding responsible decision-making in ethical and lifestyle choices

   h. teaching the biblical way of conflict resolution

Goals

• The young person will know she is created in God's image and therefore valuable and significant. She will understand this significance is what matters, not that obtained from clothes, dates, grades, etc.

• He will understand that sin is knowing what's right and not doing it. He will know that God's gracious love forgives and restores him to God when he asks.

• She will develop personal and corporate spiritual practices, including prayer, reflection, and regular participation in congregational worship.

• He will be grounded in hope built on faith, allowing him to live in joyful appreciation of each day of this life as well as anticipation of the life yet to come.

• She will make a personal commitment to Christ, unite with the church through baptism, and develop a sensitivity and appreciation for the Holy Spirit's involvement in her life.

• He will know his whole being is a "temple of the Holy Spirit" and understand the importance of nourishing his physical and emotional well-being, avoiding those lifestyle choices that hurt and destroy.

• She will be able to understand what is important for happiness and a meaningful existence, and what is non-essential. (Needs versus wants.)

2. To grow as communities of grace, joy, and peace we want to invite all youth to be an integral part of congregational life.

As we:

• call and nurture congregational leaders for ministry in a changing environment

• practice love, forgiveness, and hospitality that affirm our diversity and heal our brokenness

By:

a. creating a loving and supportive environment

b. strengthening family life

c. embracing God's gifts of multicultural and intergenerational diversity

d. advocating for youth in church and society

e. calling youth to invest themselves in building up the church

Goals

• The young person will enjoy relationships with persons of all ages, and value the wisdom that older persons can offer in the decisions she faces.

• He will learn skills that will help him work through conflicts with family, peers, and others. These skills will also help him understand conflict between nations and ideologies.

• She will learn good communication skills that she will use with family members, peers, and sisters and brothers in her church.

3. To live as people of healing and hope we are committed to call forth the gifts in youth and empower them to minister through the power of the Holy Spirit.

As we:

• invite others to faith in Jesus Christ

• seek God's peace in our homes, work, neighborhoods and the world

By:

a. seeking, recognizing, affirming and involving gifts and talents of youth

b. calling youth to share their faith

c. inviting youth to a lifestyle of missions and service

d. educating, equipping, enabling and empowering youth to minister

e. partnering with our denominational institutions and organizations to provide opportunities for ministry and missions

f. walking with youth as they live out their faith

Goals

• The young person will learn the story of God's repeated attempts to be in relationship with humankind through study of the scriptures and of the history of the Christian church.

• She will learn the story of our Anabaptist forbears. She will also learn about other religious traditions and how they compare to her Anabaptist/believers' church tradition.

• He will see himself as part of the global family, integrally connected to all peoples of the earth in the struggle for survival and happiness.

• She will develop an appreciation for the world in which she lives and discern how to be a good caretaker and manager of God's resources. This will include stewardship of her financial and personal resources.

• He will discern his gifts and God's calling for him in terms of education, vocation, service.

APPENDIX B

The 1988 Youth Ministry Team Model

DEPENDING on the size of a congregation's team, the entire team should meet anywhere from one to four times a year to plan and brainstorm about the youth ministry needs and goals of the congregation. Then the team chairperson (a youth pastor if the church has one) would keep in touch with the representatives from each area to see how things are going, as well as head up a nucleus of 3-4 people to work on details and plans during the year. Areas of responsibility to be covered by the team include:

1. *Determining needs* of the youth as a whole and of individuals. One way to do this would be to draw a large map with the church's meetinghouse in the center and each youth's name approximately where he or she lives. Listed beside each name would be information such as family members, church, school, and community involvements, and any concerns of particular interest. This map would remain in confidence among the group, and would be used to get a handle on the needs of each young person in the congregation.

2. *Determining expectations of the congregation.* What are the felt needs and goals that the congregation has for its youth? Is service a priority? Understanding Anabaptist history? Decide which goals to focus on, and how. Set the goals on a yearly basis, and word them so they are attainable in a year's time.

3. *Settings.* Not all congregations will use all of the settings described in chapter 7. It will be up to the youth ministry team to work with the settings that fit their congregation and to give leadership and support for the people leading those settings.

4. *Content and focus.* When the group has established its goals for the year, talk about how to reach those goals. Decide Sunday school curriculum, youth group input, planned events with the rest of the

church, a service trip, catechism content, and youth involvement in worship. One of the most important aspects of this team meeting is the ability to *coordinate* what's happening with the youth, rather than each setting doing its own thing. Curriculum in Sunday school might be followed up with mentor pairs discussing the same topic. A youth group trip might be to visit the congregation's sister church in another state or province. A Wednesday evening adult class might study the same topic the youth are studying in youth group—the two groups could "compare notes" together at the end of the series.

5. *Budget.* Fundraising has been both bane and blessing for youth groups through the years. Some youth groups tithe a portion of the funds they raise back to the congregational budget as a way of acknowledging their relationship with the church. A few congregations include the entire youth program in the congregation's budget. Any funds raised by the youth become part of the congregation's budget and youth ministry costs are paid through it. Youth are strongly encouraged to pledge a tithe of their personal income as contributions to the congregation.

6. *Support for youth leaders.* The youth ministry team is a sounding board for those who work with youth—a place to share concerns, problems, and joys. This is one means of support the team provides. Another one is to make available leadership-training and spiritual events for those in leadership. The team could send the youth sponsors to a spiritual retreat for a weekend, or pay the way for the Sunday school teachers to attend a resourcing event. This kind of support means a lot to volunteers who may sometimes feel that their efforts go unnoticed and unappreciated.

7. *Evaluation.* The youth ministry team should evaluate what's happening in the various settings every 1-2 years. This means providing a questionnaire and/or talking with the youth for feedback. It may also be helpful to bring in an outside resource person to help with the evaluation.

8. *Reporting to the congregation.* Whether through articles in the church newsletter, a report in the annual report book, sharing during the congregational worship, a bulletin board, or all of the above, the youth ministry team needs to inform the congregation of what's happening in youth ministry. Through being informed the congregation will take more ownership in this important program.

Youth and Young Adult Ministry

by Jonathan Neufeld and Doug Klassen*

I. Youth and Young Adult Initiative Team

A. Definition: The Initiative Team works together to set the congregation's direction for youth and young adult ministry. It identifies purpose and mission, formulates policy, and discerns leadership.

B. Composition: This team shall consist of three members that are elected by the congregation.

    1. Congregational Youth and Young Adult Ministry Representative (CMR)

    2. A parent of a junior or senior high youth

    3. A youth or young adult

       The associate pastor or youth pastor is an ex officio member of the team.

       One of the three positions shall be filled by election each year.

C. Objectives

    1. To work on the congregation's vision for God's work with youth and young adults, and to discern new ministry initiatives.

    2. To be a voice to the congregation with regards to youth and young adult issues, concerns, and ministries.

    3. To nurture the ministry leaders of Impulse Centers. The primary context for this nurture will be the quarterly services of sharing and worship, called Youth and Young Adults: Ministry That Matters.

---

* Adapted, with permission, from the course "Youth and Family Ministry Into the 21st Century" taught by Roland D. Martinson, May 27-June 1, 1996, at Canadian Mennonite Bible College.

4. To be active in discerning gifts, considering people who could be invited to be part of Youth and Young Adult Ministry.

II. Impulse Centers

The hands-on work of youth and young adult ministry is accomplished by persons of particular gifts and a variety of responsibilities throughout the congregation. These program or task committees become as numerous as is needed to carry out the congregation's youth and young adult ministry activities. For example, there might be a junior youth impulse center, a retreat impulse center, a young adult Bible study impulse center or a service trip impulse center. The number of impulse centers established will depend on the extent of the program and the availability of volunteers. The leaders of these centers shall be appointed by church council based on the recommendation of the initiative team.

III. Youth and Young Adults: Ministry That Matters

A. Definition: Youth and Young Adults: Ministry That Matters is a quarterly (could also be semi-annual or annual) gathering for ministry workers to be nurtured through worship, inspired through prayer, and encouraged through sharing; provides the context in which ministry leaders can be a nurturing community.

B. Composition: The group consists of the Initiative Team and the leaders from the Impulse Centers.

C. Objectives

1. To provide the setting for worship, sharing, rejuvenation, and the discussion of significant ministry issues.
2. To facilitate communication between the Impulse Centers.

IV. Roles

A. *The Congregational Youth and Young Adult Ministry Representative (CMR)* is in charge of the Youth and Young Adult Ministry (YaYA) on behalf of the congregation. It's the CMR's responsibility to initiate conversation with the Initiative Team about the nature of the congregation's ministry with youth and young adults. Together they design the processes and formulate the strategies to shape this ministry. The Initiative Team meets monthly to build trust and address the tasks at hand. The CMR is a member of the church council and chair person of the Initiative Team. Deep faith, commitment to congregational ministry, administrative ability, and access to the political power of the church are crucial attributes of the CMR. The CMR leads the Initiative Team as it discerns policies, vision, and strategies, and implements them in the congregation. The CMR takes initiative, guiding and advocating on behalf of youth and youth adults in the congregation and community. The CMR is the primary congregational leader in youth ministry.

B. *The Initiative Team* works together in setting the congregation's direction for youth and young adult ministry—-identifying purpose and mission, formulating policy, and discerning leadership. This team advocates youth and young adult concerns, develops leadership, and oversees the Impulse Centers. It does not do the hands-on work with YaYA; rather, it reviews ministry objectives and covenants, keeping the Impulse Centers accountable. This team nurtures the Impulse Center leaders by organizing the annual (or more often if so desired) worship services called Youth and Young Adults: Ministry That Matters. This team is guided by three basic questions: Among youth and young adults, (1) Where is God active? How are we participating in this activity? (2) Where is God active and we do not participate? (3) Where should we become more active?

C. *Associate Pastor/Youth Pastor* joins this team as a theological and ministerial consultant. The pastor brings expertise in theological inquiry and formulation, and adds breadth gained from participation in the larger ministry of the church. It is this person's responsibility to thoroughly know the youth and young adults and the YaYA ministry activities of the congregation. This person should be trained and experienced in youth ministry. The pastor will also work with the Impulse Center leaders to formulate ministry objectives, bringing the ministry leaders to be dedicated on Education Sunday. The pastor and the Initiative Team support each other in their work with the ministry leaders and church council.

D. *Impulse Centers* are where the hands-on work of the youth and young adult ministry occur. The persons leading these centers are of all ages and have a variety of characteristics and capabilities.

Most importantly, they possess a lively faith and a commitment to ministry. These persons are identified and secured by the Initiative Team. Each volunteer will be asked to complete a covenant of responsibility with the Initiative Team, as worked out with the associate pastor of youth. This covenant will outline the ministry objectives of the leader, and what the associate pastor and Initiative Team promise to do for them. The purpose of the covenanting process is to ensure that the volunteer can be held accountable, and so that the volunteer is not abused by a growing list of responsibilities throughout the year.

E. *Suggested Monthly Agenda for Initiative Team*
  1. Narrate the Now
     • Process what is happening in the ministry
     • Talk about the big picture
     • Compare with the larger mission of the congregation
     • Where did youth begin? Direction?
     • Strengths and weaknesses—emphasize the strengths
  2. What Is God Up To?
     • What is the gospel message?
     • Where is God's presence and activity?
     • What does God want to do in our church?
     • What does God need done in our community?
     • What does this look like in ministry—in word and in worship
  3. Community Outreach
     • What are the concerns of our community?
     • Are people hurting?
     • What is God's dream for these people?

Spiritual Formation Model

by Mark Yaconelli*

I. The Leadership Team

In instructing our youth ministry I wanted to be careful not to create a separate community of youth and young adults who had little interaction with the sponsoring church. To insure that the youth ministry would represent the spirituality of our church community, I gathered seven adults from different groupings within our church—a retired banker, an office manager in her 30s, a dad with three kids under eleven, a single mom with two teenagers, a young man in his 20s who plays rock-n-roll on the weekends, a new mom in her 30s, one of our copastors, and myself. I asked these people to serve as a "covenant group" whose primary purpose is discernment.

The adult leaders team is committed to meeting each week for an hour before youth group to pray, read Scripture, discuss experiences of God within our own lives and within the lives of the youth group members, and to listen for what programs God is calling us to create. Finally, the group seeks to use the team meetings as a time to nurture our own commitment and discipleship to Jesus Christ within the context of ministering to youth.

II. A Typical Leadership Meeting

Opening Prayer—usually involves some time for silence.

Check-in—a brief opportunity for people to communicate the baggage they bring to the meeting.

Lectio Divina—After a time of silence, a biblical passage is read two or three times (we often use a passage that reflects the theme

---

* From the Winter 1998 issue of *Chimes* (Volume 43, Number 1), a quarterly magazine published by San Francisco Theological Seminary. Used with permission.

for the evening's youth meeting). Team members listen for a word or phrase that "shimmers" or "sticks." After a few more minutes of silence each member shares the word or image and what it means for them in their own life of faith. (At times we do lectio on statements, prayers, or artwork by youth as a process for staying attentive to God's presence in the youth group.)

Openings and Blocks—One team member shares "openings" (where he or she sensed God's presence of movement in the youth group the previous week) and "blocks" (where God's movement felt blocked or shut out). This is followed by prayerful reflections by the rest of the group.

Assignments/Planning—Every other week we spend a longer time noticing the various openings and how they may inform our programming and planning.

Closing Prayer—Offering up gratitude and listening for common themes in the meeting.

After a year and a half of working with this leadership format we've discovered four distinct ways in which our meetings have become beneficial to the youth.

1. *Preparation:* By engaging in biblical meditation, silence, and other contemplative prayer practices, we've discovered the leadership meetings draw our attention to God's activity rather than to our own performance anxieties. Through this new focus we've begun to trust and understand that the ministry belongs to God. We've noticed that we no longer feel pressure that the success of the ministry depends on our own spiritual achievements; we sense a new freedom to welcome and minister to young people.

2. *Transformation:* When reflecting on our experience of God in the youth group we often come into contact with our own spiritual longings. We use the team meetings as a place to share and nurture these longings, believing that our desires for God can be our greatest gift to young people. Through "praying the ministry" we're discovering that the youth group is not solely about kids encountering God—we too are being changed by this ministry.

3. *Discernment:* Whereas previously we planned youth programs for the whole year and then asked God to bless them, we now listen for what God is doing and then respond according to our discernment. We've encountered a deeper companionship with the

Holy Spirit as we've sought to respond and work alongside the Spirit's gentle nurturing. We've also been surprised and grateful to see how effective our programs have become and watched as many of the students have expressed significant growth in faith and practice.

4. *Call:* The leadership team meetings have helped us to hear our call. We've begun to notice the ways in which our individual calls are woven together to serve youth. Together we're discovering a shared vision of faith and ministry that is encouraging and nurturing to all of us. We are continually amazed at how paying attention to our call in youth ministry informs us about God's invitations in other areas of our lives. We continually reflect on how youth ministry has become a spiritual discipline—a practice that helps us deepen our own intimacy with the holy.

III. Leadership as Discipleship

These team meetings have allowed volunteers and myself to continue to serve in youth ministry with a sense of joy and expectation. We leave youth meetings encouraged and renewed rather than burned out. We look forward to our leadership gatherings rather than look for excuses to get out of another boring committee meeting. Most importantly, we are living out the Christian life in a way that is real and visible to young people. We no longer speak to youth of the importance of the Christian faith without experiencing its wonder and power. Seeking the movement of God, we are eager to invite youth to join us in listening for that still small voice that calls out, "I have come that you may have life, and have it abundantly."

Starting a Mentoring Program

by Chris Douglas*

How we started our mentoring program

- Ask youth
- Recruit adult mentors that youth chose
- Commissioning/recognition during worship
- Training session
- Mentor contact accountability

Maybe you've been like me: I'd read about other churches' mentoring programs and even recommended it to people looking for more effective ministry with youth. But I hadn't tried it yet myself. My opportunity came when my congregation asked me to begin a mentoring program for our local church, both junior and senior high youth. Here's how we set it up:

We sent letters to 21 youth explaining the new mentoring program (an addition to our regular youth group activities). Along with the letter went a form where they could indicate whether or not they were interested, and if so, to write the name of their first three choices of adults as mentors. We got only a few responses, so we phoned each youth. Eventually, 12 youth named adults they wanted as mentors. As you might expect, most of these were the busiest adults in our congregation. As mentoring coordinator, I went to each of those 12 adults and said, "I know you are already very busy, and taking on this commitment may mean you need to resign from one of your other church responsibilities. On behalf of our congregation, I am calling you to the ministry of mentoring one of our youth. When

---

* From *YouthGuide*, Spring 1998 (Faith & Life Press). Used by permission.

(name of youth) was asked who he or she would like for a mentor, he or she named you out of all the other adults in this entire church. Will you accept the call of the church and the desire of this youth to serve as his or her mentor for the year?" I outlined the expectations: an activity once a month with the youth, some kind of contact weekly (a phone call, a note or card in the mail, or talking together at church Sunday morning), and daily to pray for the youth. We'd have training sessions for mentors and to check in about how it's going. Occasionally, we'd have some activities for mentors and youth to all get together.

Even busy people accepted the call. We scheduled a commissioning/recognition service during worship. We held up the new mentoring program as one of the ways for the congregation to fulfill the promise of support they made to parents during child dedication years before. We first asked the parents to bless this new relationship, and then asked the mentors to commit themselves on behalf of the congregation to walk alongside these youth as they explore questions of faith and of daily living. The congregation reaffirmed their support in raising its young people to Christian maturity.

A training session was held that same week. I developed a "Mentor Contact Form" and asked each mentor to fill one out after each activity they did with their youth. It asks for date of the activity, what was done, and any reflections on it. We wanted to be sure none of the youth "fell through the cracks" after all the hype. I made a chart with the names of each pair and twelve blocks across from each name. When I receive a "Mentor Contact Form" I note the date of that activity on the chart, so it's easy to keep track of any relationships that seem to be lagging in contact. It takes a little more time, but it helps insure that regular contacts are happening. We have high hopes for what our mentoring program will mean in terms of quality of relationships and what difference it will make in the lives of youth in our congregation.

Chris Douglas is also United States staff person for Youth and Young Adult Ministries in the Church of the Brethren.

Building Together

Recommended Reading

Benson, Peter. *The Troubled Journey*. Minneapolis: Search Institute, 1990.

Bibby, Reginald W., and Donald C. Posterski. *Teen Trends: A Nation in Motion*. Toronto: Stoddart Publishing, 1992.

Bogard, Mike. *41 Ways to a Better Youth Group*. Newton: Faith & Life Press, 1996.

Borgman, Dean. *When Kumbaya Is Not Enough: A Practical Theology for Youth Ministry*. Peabody: Hendrickson Publishers, 1997.

Dean, Kenda Creasy and Ron Foster. *The Godbearing Life: The Art of Soul Tending for Youth Ministry*. Upper Room Books: Nashville, Tenn., 1998.

Dean, Kenda Creasy, Chap Clark, and Dave Rahn, ed. *Starting Right: Thinking Theologically About Youth Ministry*. Grand Rapids: Zondervan, 2001.

Fields, Doug. *Purpose Driven Youth Ministry: 9 Essential Foundations for Healthy Growth*. Grand Rapids: Zondervan Publishing House, 1998.

Garland, Diana R. *Family Ministry: A Comprehensive Guide*. Downers Grove: InterVarsity Press, 2000.

Hyland, Terry and Ron Herron, ed. *The Ongoing Journey: Awakening Spiritual Life in At-Risk Youth*. Boys Town, Neb.: Boys Town Press, 1995.

Jones, Stephen. *Faith Shaping: Youth and the Experience of Faith*. Valley Forge: Judson Press, 1987.

Roland D. Martinson. *Effective Youth Ministry: A Congregational Approach*. Minneapolis: Augsburg, 1988.

Mueller, Walt. *Understanding Today's Youth Culture*. Wheaton: Tyndale House Publishers, 1994.

Neff, Blake. J., and Donald Ratcliff, ed. *Handbook of Family Religious Education*. Birmingham: Religious Education Press, 1995.

Nelson, C. Ellis. *Helping Teenagers Grow Morally*. Louisville: Westminster/John Knox Press, 1992.

Ratcliff, Donald and James A. Davies, ed. *Handbook of Youth Ministry*. Birmingham: Religious Education Press, 1991.

Robbins, Duffy. *The Ministry of Nurture*. Grand Rapids: Zondervan, 1990.

Roehlkepartain, Eugene C., Elanah Dalyah Naftali, and Laura Musegades. *Growing Up Generous: Engaging Youth in Giving and Serving*. Bethesda: The Alban Institute, 2000.

Senter III, Mark H., ed. *Four Views of Youth Ministry and the Church: Inclusive Congregational, Preparatory, Missional, Strategic*. Grand Rapids: Zondervan, 2001.

Shelton, Charles. *Adolescent Spirituality*. Chicago: Loyola University Press, 1983.

Strommen, Merton P. *Five Cries of Youth*. San Francisco: Harper & Row, 1988.

Strommen, Merton P., and Richard A. Hardel. *Passing on the Faith: A Radical New Model for Youth and Family Ministry*. Winona: Saint Mary's Press, 2000.

Thompson, Marjorie J. *Family: The Forming Center*. Nashville: Upper Room Books, 1996.

Trimmer, Edward A. *Youth Ministry Handbook*. Nashville: Abingdon Press, 1994.

Warren, Michael. *Youth, Gospel, Liberation*. San Francisco: Harper & Row, 1987.